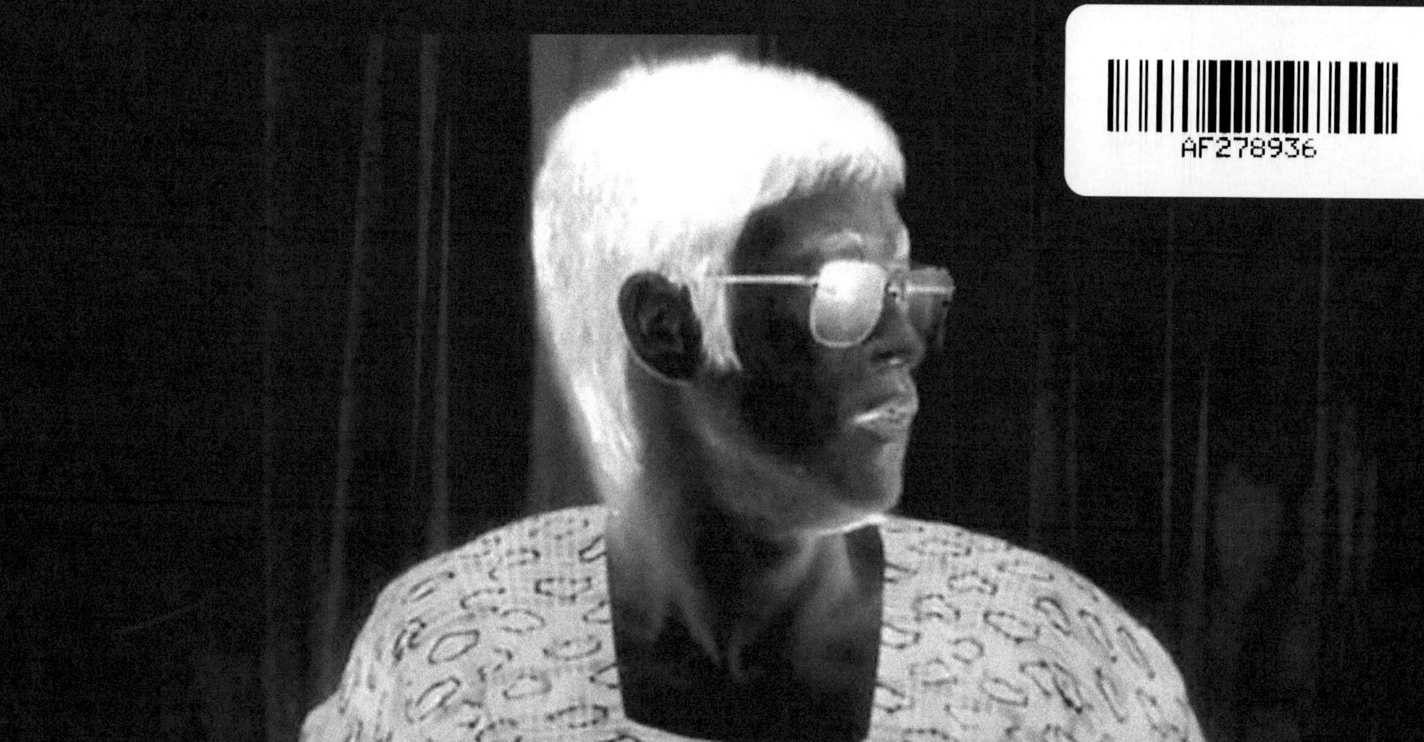

BRUCE LEE, RENOWNED FOR HIS GROUNDBREAKING CONTRIBUTIONS TO MARTIAL ARTS AND CINEMA, WAS NOT JUST A MASTER OF PHYSICAL COMBAT; HE WAS ALSO A VIRTUOSO OF FACIAL EXPRESSION. FROM HIS EARLY DAYS AS A CHILD ACTOR IN HONG KONG TO HIS METEORIC RISE AS A GLOBAL MARTIAL ARTS SUPERSTAR, LEE DEMONSTRATED AN EXTRAORDINARY ABILITY TO CONVEY A WIDE SPECTRUM OF EMOTIONS WITHOUT UTTERING A SINGLE WORD. THIS SKILL, BLENDING SEAMLESSLY WITH HIS ON-SCREEN FIGHTING PROWESS, HAS CEMENTED HIS LEGACY AS A MULTIFACETED PERFORMER.

AS A CHILD ACTOR, LEE'S EXPRESSIVE FACE WAS ALREADY A PROMINENT FEATURE OF HIS PERFORMANCES. HIS YOUTHFUL EXUBERANCE AND INNATE CHARM SHONE THROUGH IN FILMS LIKE "THE KID" (1950). EVEN AT A YOUNG AGE, LEE EXHIBITED A REMARKABLE ABILITY TO CONVEY INNOCENCE, JOY, AND CURIOSITY, DRAWING AUDIENCES INTO HIS WORLD WITH JUST A GLANCE OR A SMILE. THIS EARLY EXPOSURE TO THE INTRICACIES OF ACTING LAID A STRONG FOUNDATION FOR THE MORE COMPLEX EMOTIONAL EXPRESSIONS HE WOULD LATER MASTE

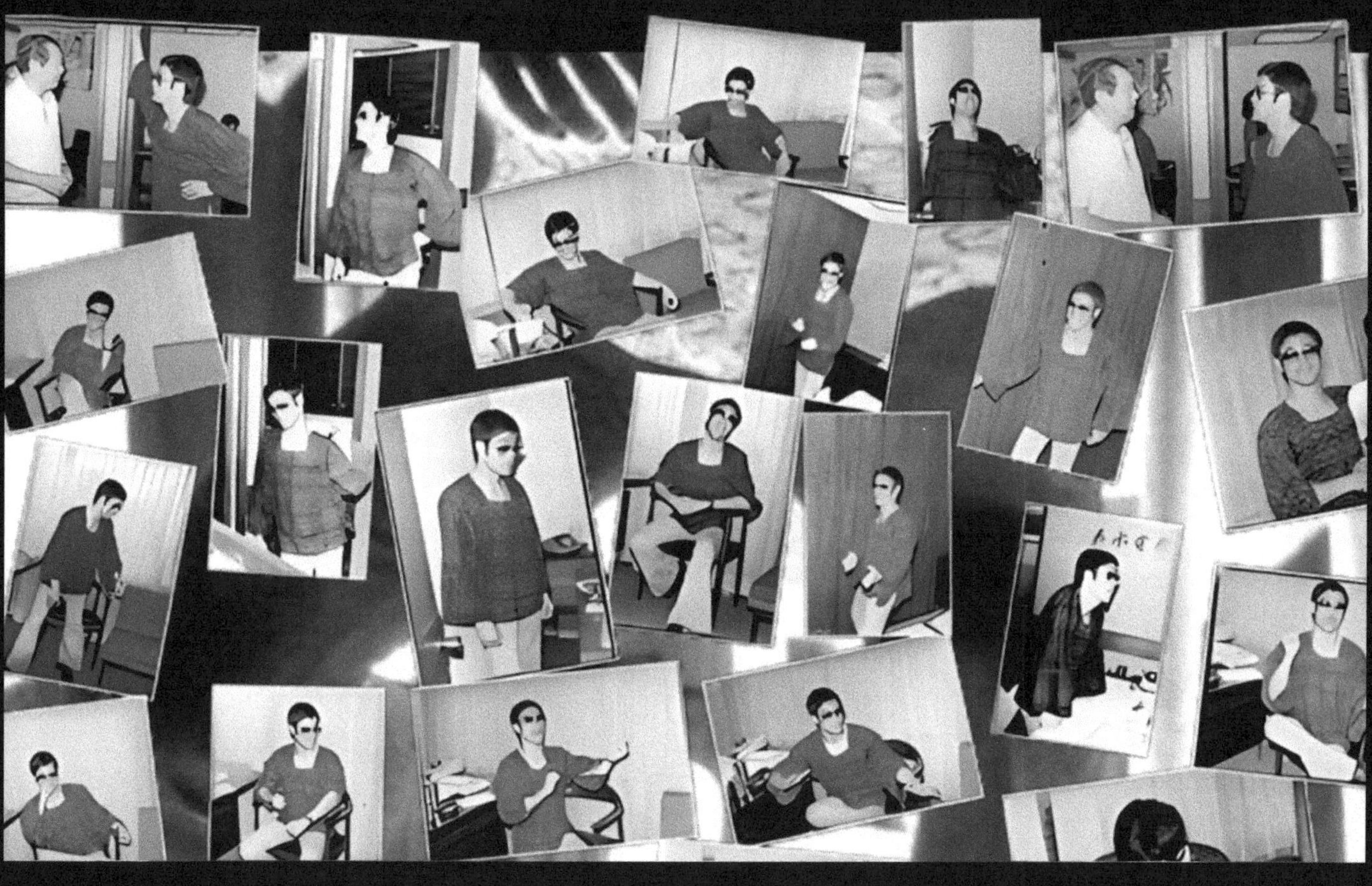

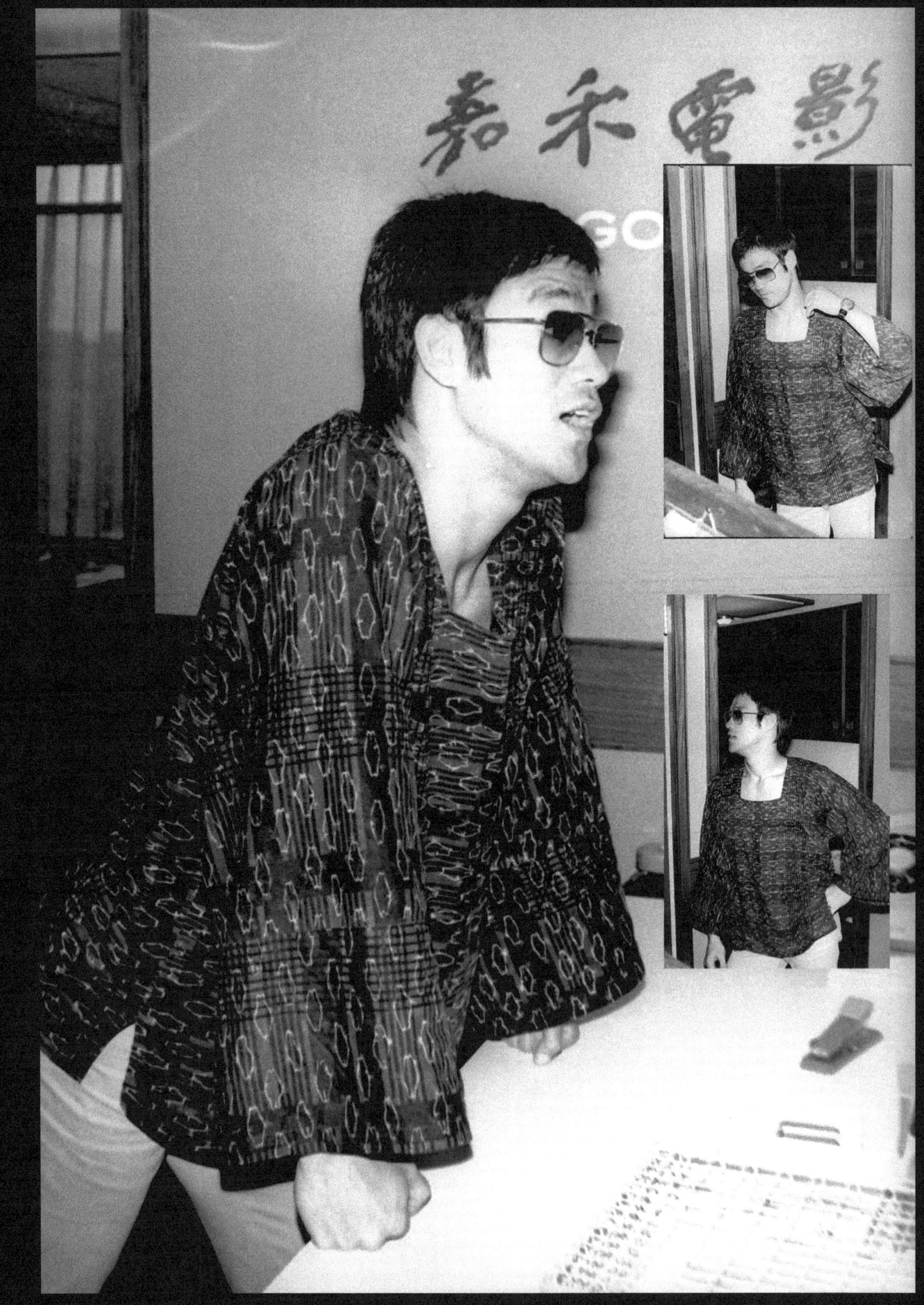

嘉禾電影
GO

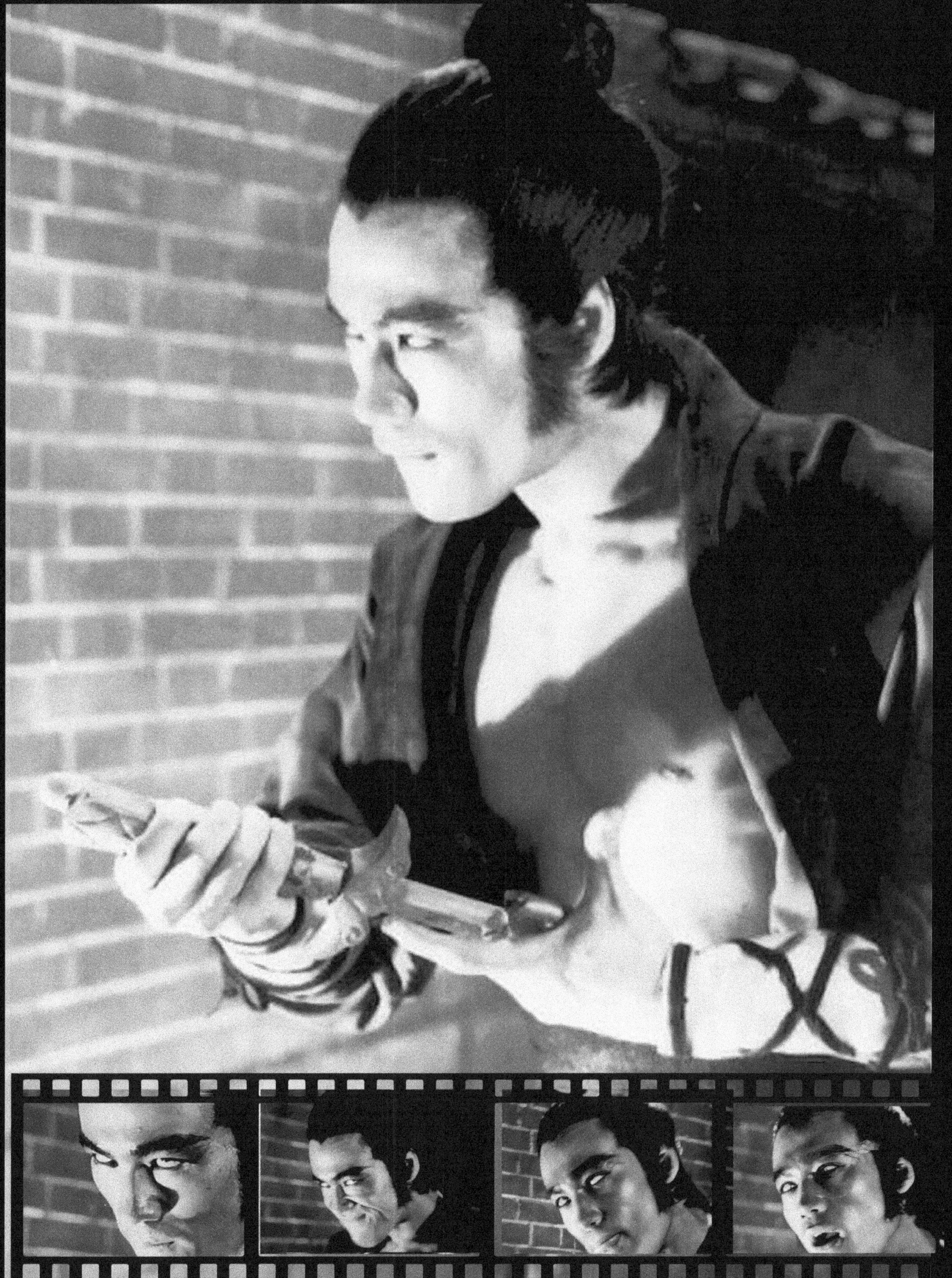

"TRUE VISION IS NOT DEFINED BY SIGHT, BUT BY THE CLARITY OF ONE'S MIND AND THE STRENGTH OF ONE'S SPIRIT." –
BRUCE LEE

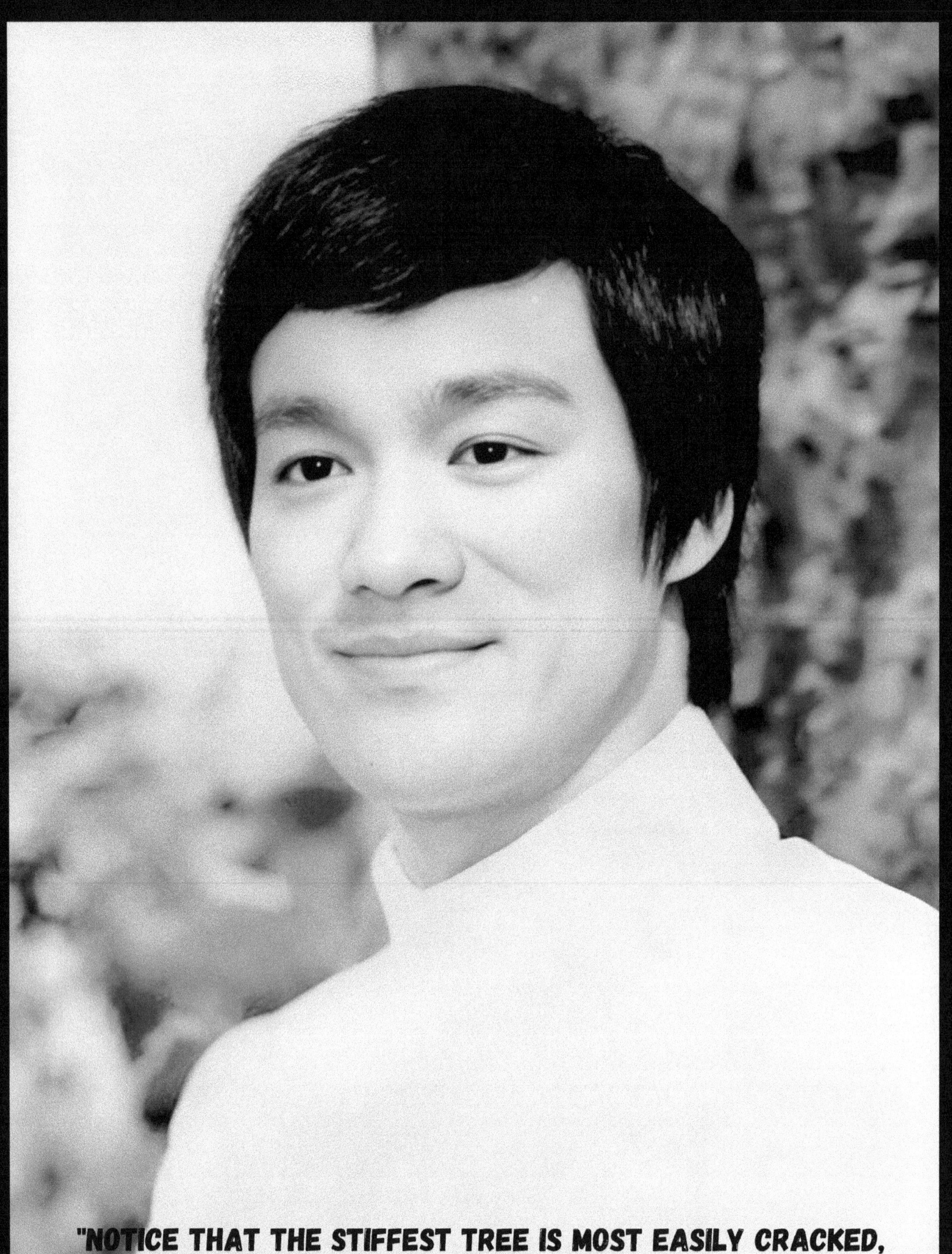

"NOTICE THAT THE STIFFEST TREE IS MOST EASILY CRACKED,
WHILE THE BAMBOO OR WILLOW SURVIVES BY BENDING WITH THE WIND.

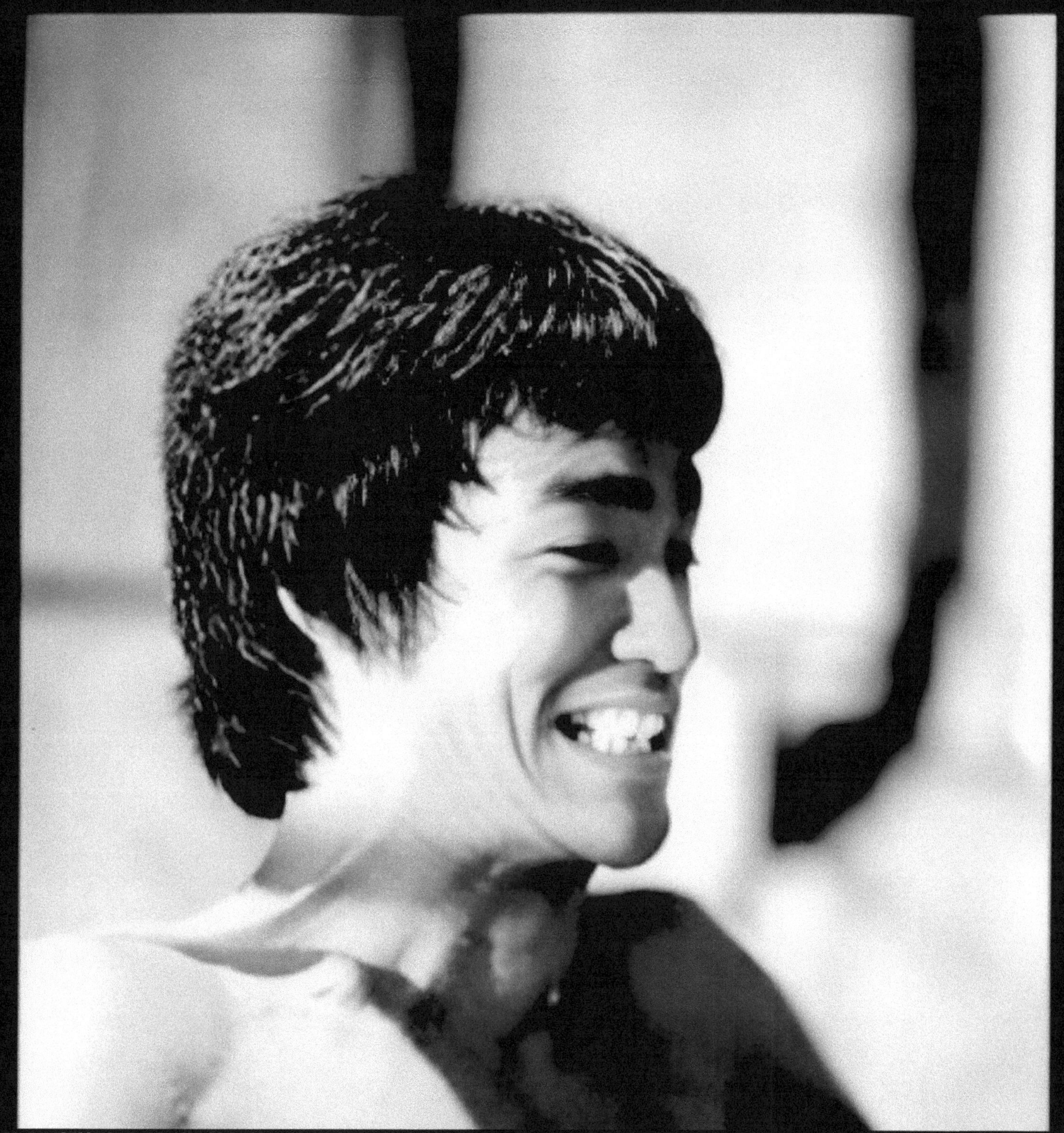

TRANSITIONING TO HIS ICONIC ROLES IN MARTIAL ARTS CINEMA, LEE'S FACE BECAME A CANVAS FOR A VAST ARRAY OF EMOTIONS, EACH ONE AS IMPACTFUL AS HIS LIGHTNING-FAST KICKS AND PUNCHES. HIS PLEASANT SMILE, OFTEN SEEN IN MOMENTS OF CAMARADERIE OR TRIUMPH, WAS WARM AND INFECTIOUS, REVEALING A SIDE OF LEE THAT WAS BOTH RELATABLE AND ENDEARING. THIS SMILE, DISARMING AND GENUINE, CONTRASTED SHARPLY WITH THE INTENSITY HE DISPLAYED DURING COMBAT SCENES, SHOWCASING HIS VERSATILITY AS AN ACTOR.

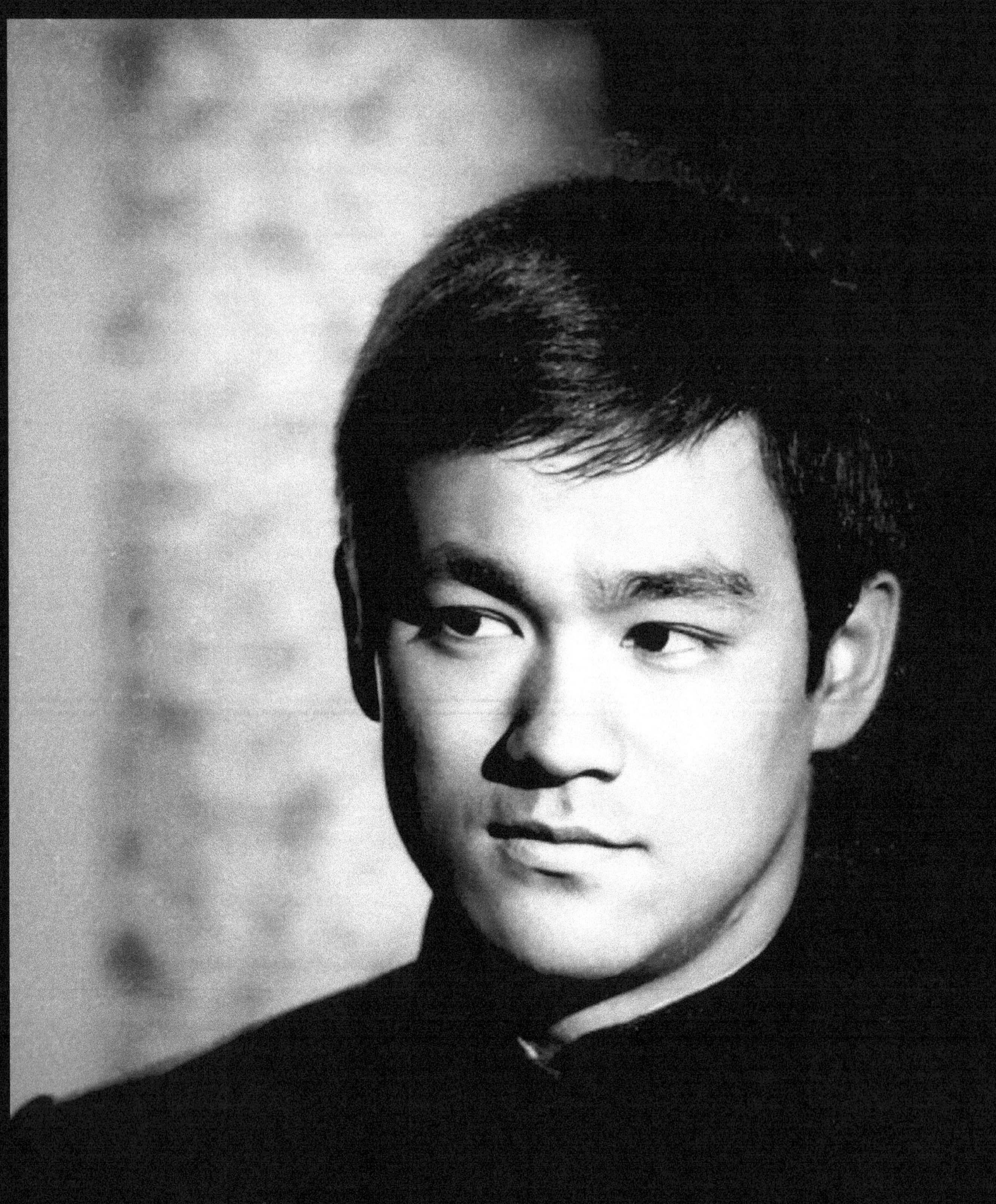

BRUCE LEE'S BOYISH GOOD LOOKS HELPED HIM LAND THE ROLE OF KATO IN "THE GREEN HORNET." HOWEVER, ONCE HIS MASK WAS ON, HE TRANSFORMED INTO A LETHAL FIGHTING MACHINE.

FACIAL EXPRESSIONS

BRUCE LEE'S FACE WAS REMARKABLY EXPRESSIVE DURING CONVERSATIONS. HIS EXPRESSIONS RANGED FROM INTENSE FOCUS TO PLAYFUL AMUSEMENT, OFTEN SHIFTING QUICKLY TO CONVEY A MULTITUDE OF EMOTIONS. WHETHER DISCUSSING MARTIAL ARTS PHILOSOPHY OR SHARING PERSONAL ANECDOTES, LEE'S EYES SPARKLED WITH PASSION AND HIS SMILE EXUDED WARMTH. HIS FURROWED BROWS AND SHARP GAZE COULD SWIFTLY TURN SERIOUS, REFLECTING DEEP CONTEMPLATION. THIS DYNAMIC RANGE OF FACIAL EXPRESSIONS MADE HIS CONVERSATIONS NOT ONLY ENGAGING BUT ALSO PROFOUNDLY INSIGHTFUL, REVEALING THE DEPTH OF HIS THOUGHTS AND THE INTENSITY OF HIS CHARACTER. LEE'S EXPRESSIVE FACE WAS A TESTAMENT TO HIS CHARISMA AND COMMUNICATIVE PROWESS.

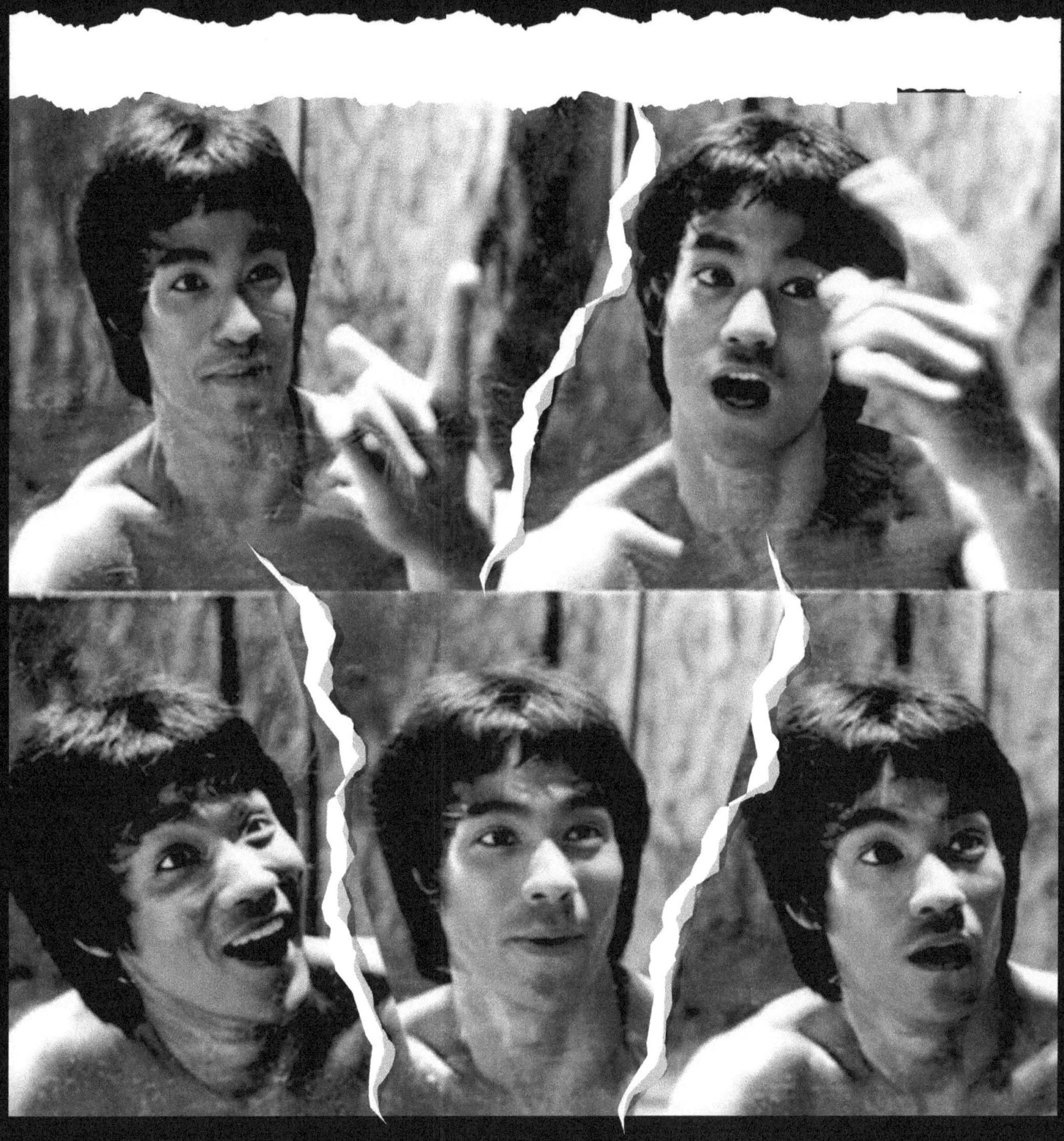

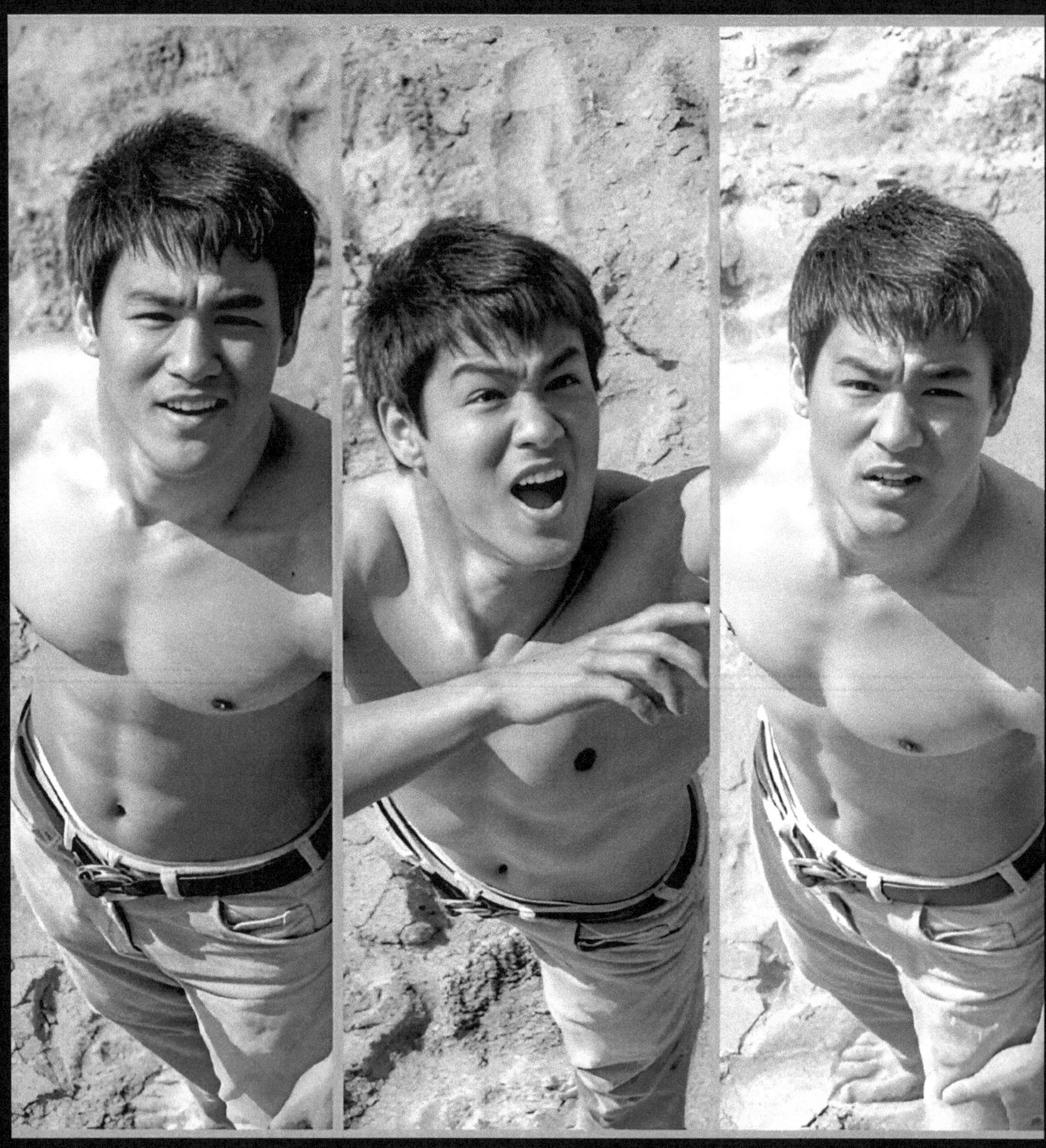

IN A RARE MOMENT OF RELAXATION, BRUCE LEE REVEALS A DIFFERENT SET OF EXPRESSIONS, SHOWING HE IS AT EASE AND ENJOYING HIS TIME OFF BETWEEN INTENSE TRAINING AND FILMING. HIS USUAL FOCUSED INTENSITY GIVES WAY TO A RELAXED DEMEANOR, EYES SOFTENING WITH A GENUINE SMILE. LOUNGING COMFORTABLY, HE APPEARS TO SAVOR THE BREAK, THE WEIGHT OF HIS RIGOROUS SCHEDULE TEMPORARILY LIFTED. HIS LAUGHTER IS UNGUARDED, HIS MOVEMENTS UNHURRIED, EMBODYING A SERENE AND JOYFUL SPIRIT. THIS GLIMPSE OF BRUCE LEE, FREE FROM HIS USUAL DISCIPLINE, HIGHLIGHTS A MAN WHO FINDS BALANCE AND JOY IN LIFE'S SIMPLE, UNSTRUCTURED MOMENTS.

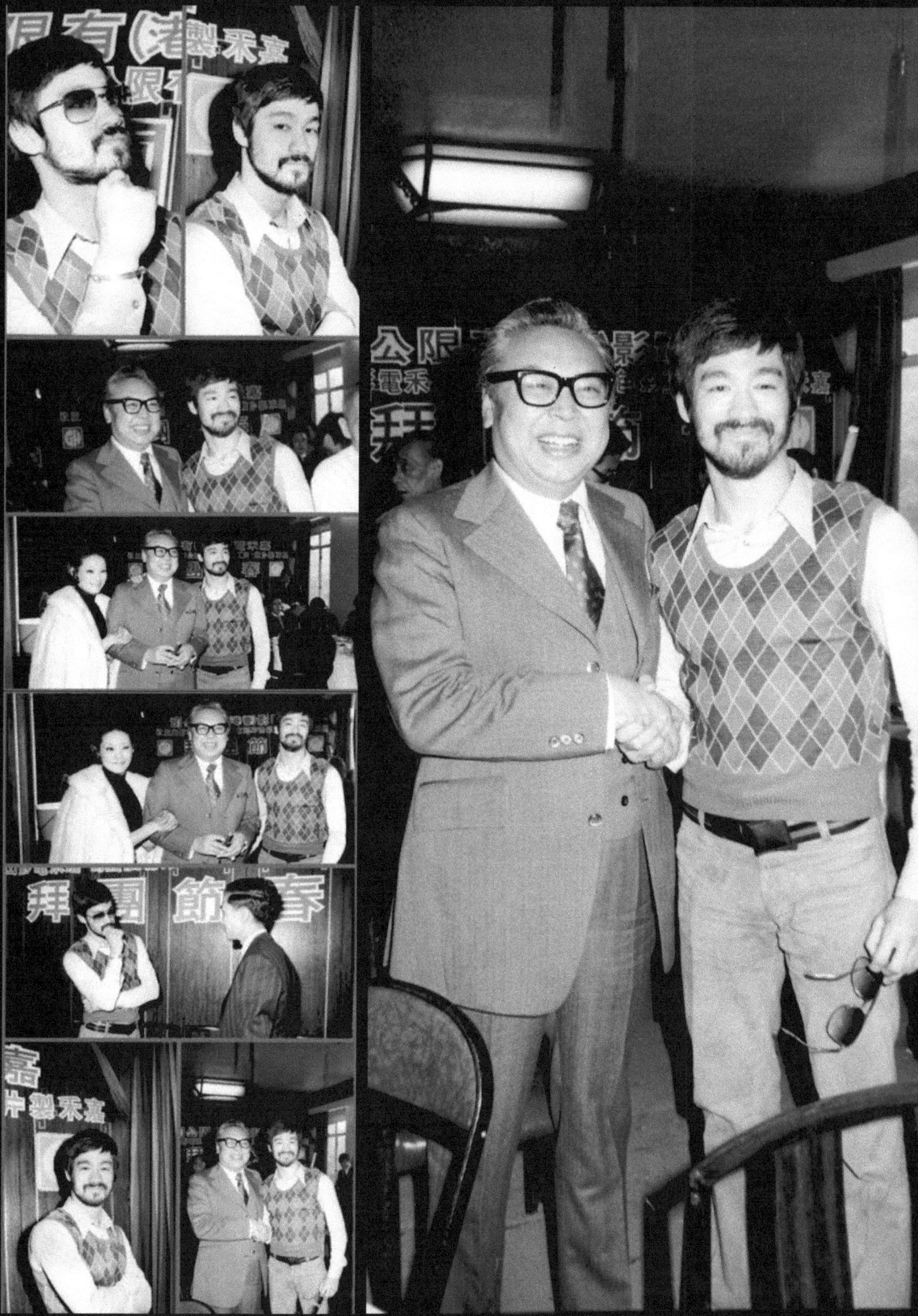

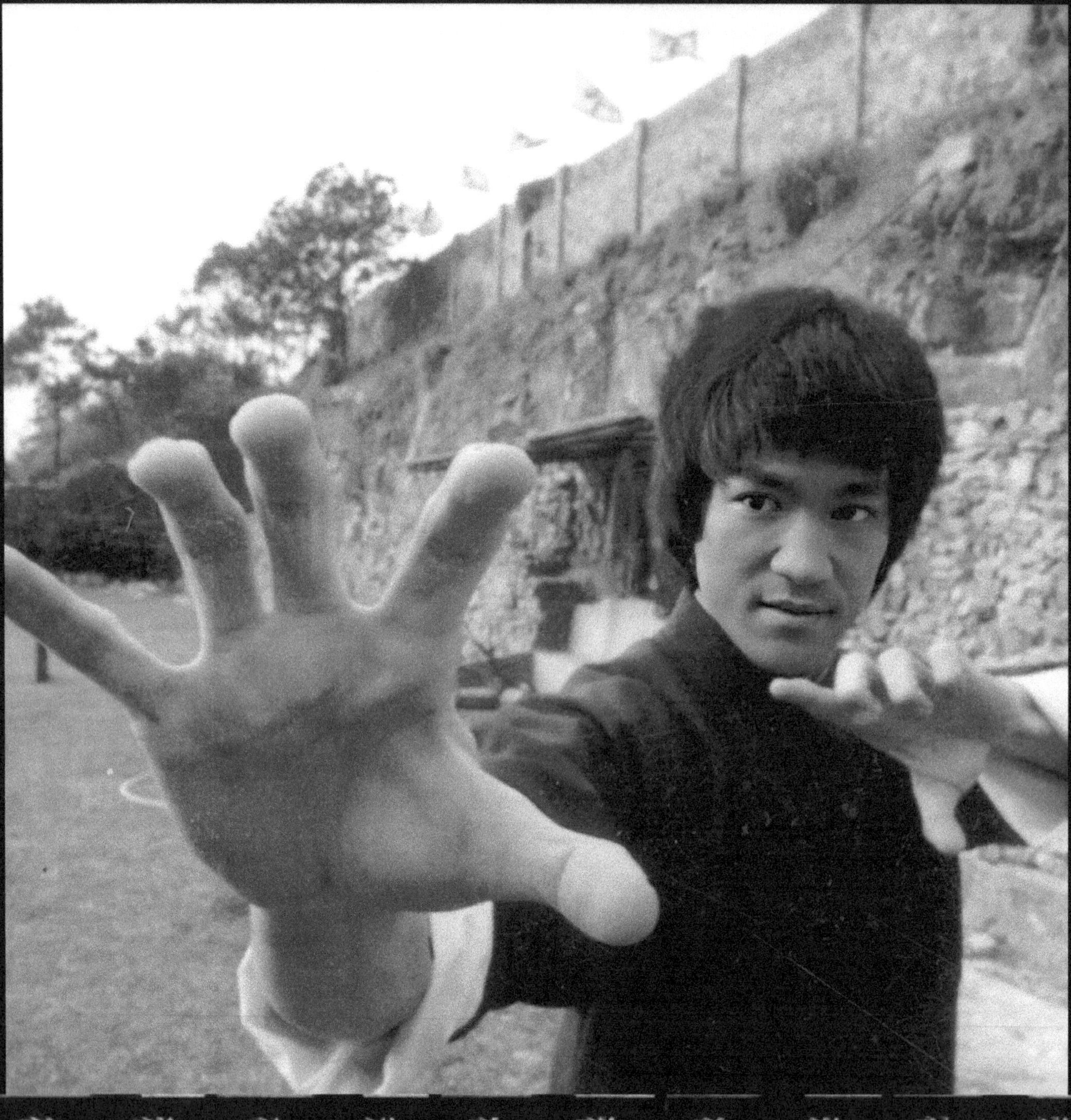

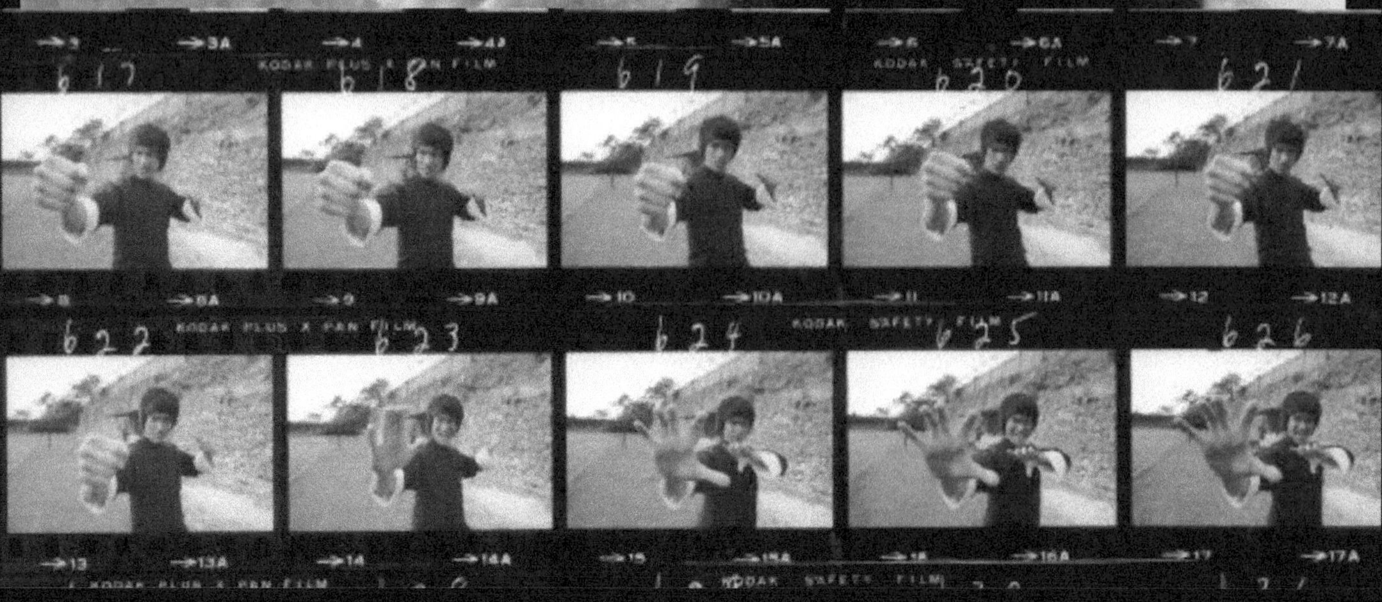

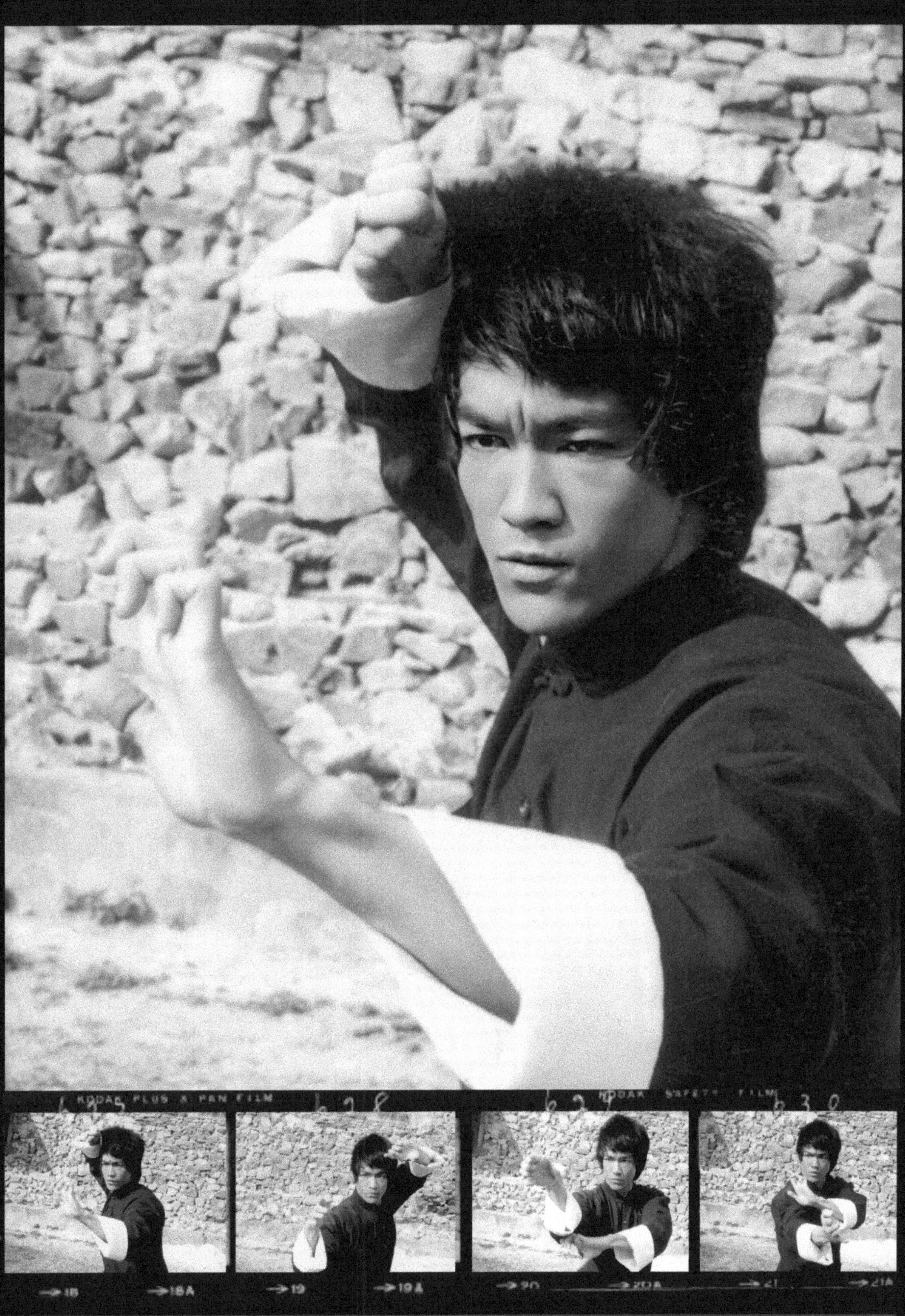

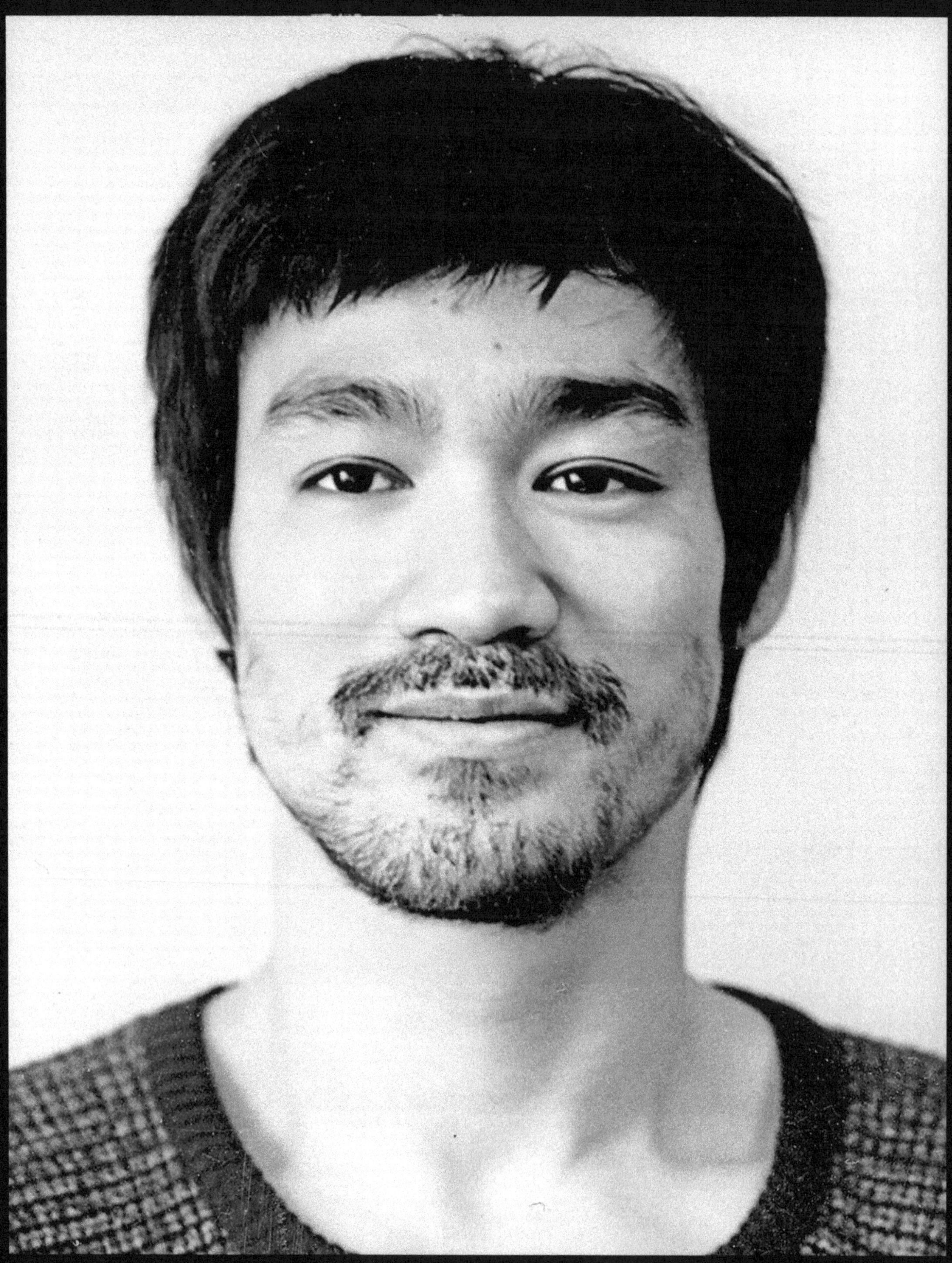

PHOTO POSE WITH LITTLE EMOTION IDEAL FOR A PASSPORT

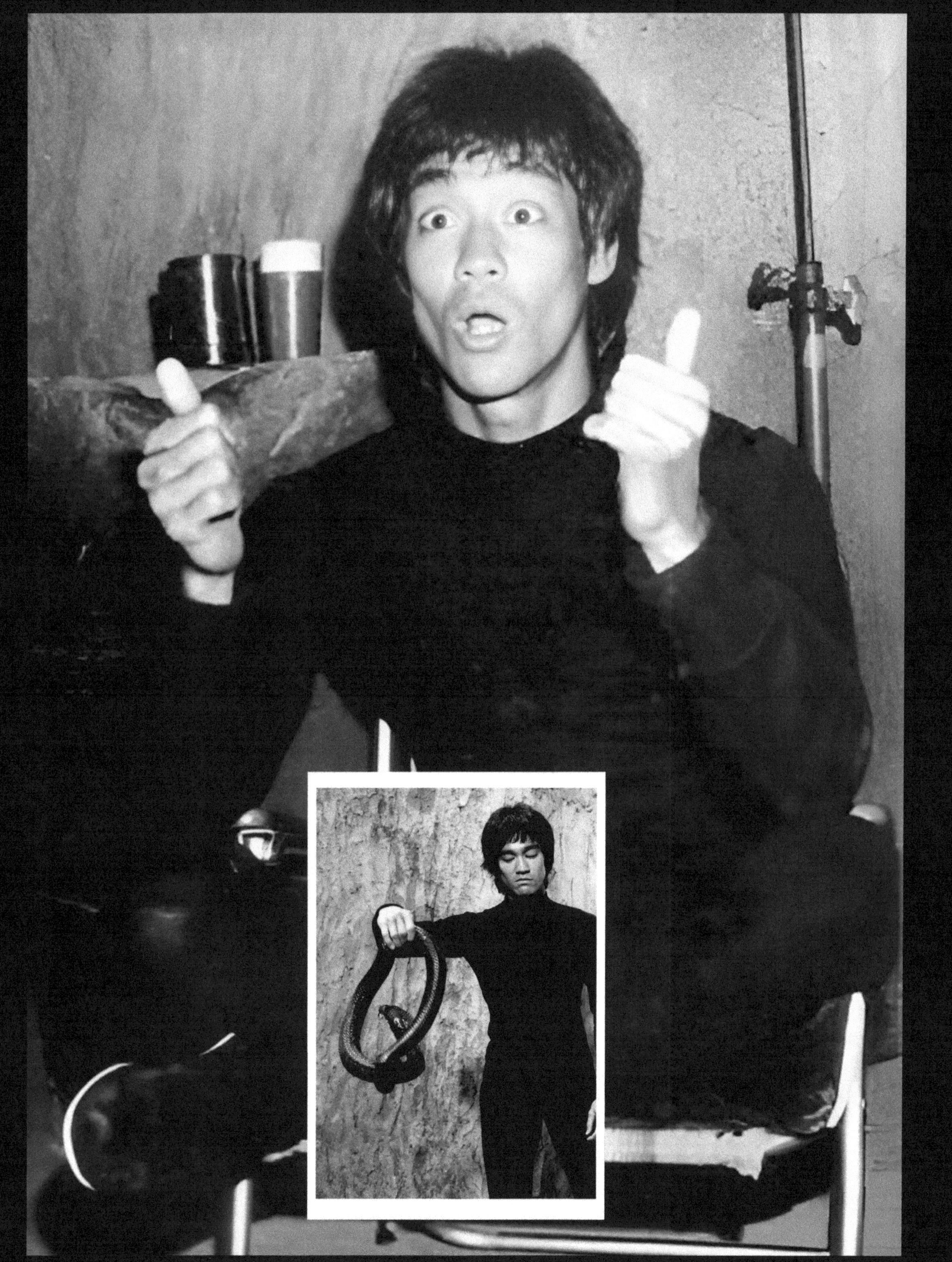

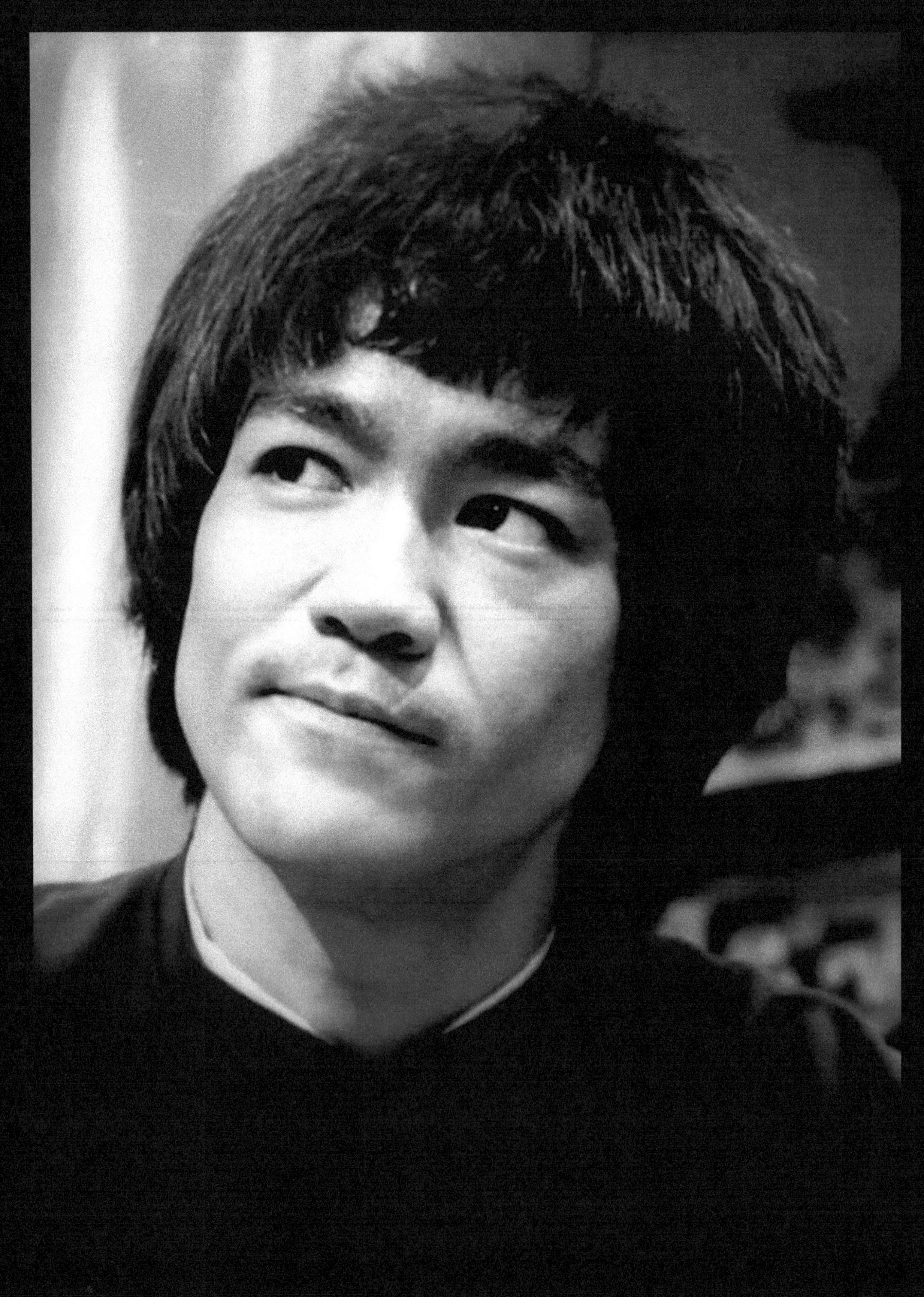

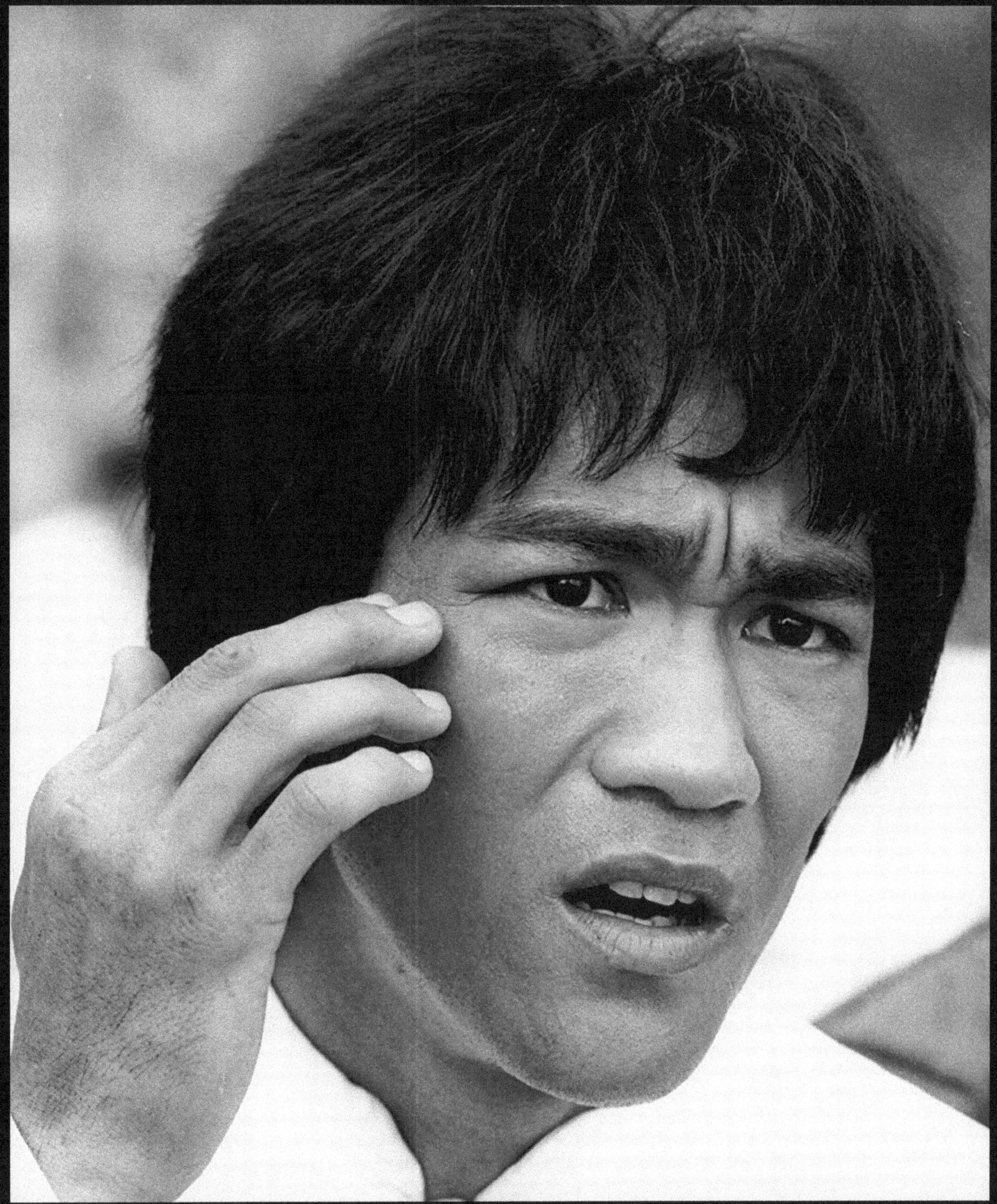

IN QUIETER MOMENTS, LEE'S FACIAL EXPRESSIONS COULD CONVEY DEEP CONTEMPLATION AND PHILOSOPHICAL INTROSPECTION. HIS ROLES OFTEN INCLUDED SCENES WHERE HE WOULD REFLECT ON THE NATURE OF MARTIAL ARTS, LIFE, AND PERSONAL GROWTH. DURING THESE SCENES, A PENSIVE FURROW OF THE BROW OR A THOUGHTFUL GAZE INTO THE DISTANCE COMMUNICATED HIS CHARACTER'S INTERNAL STRUGGLES AND INSIGHTS, ADDING LAYERS OF DEPTH TO HIS PERFORMANCES.

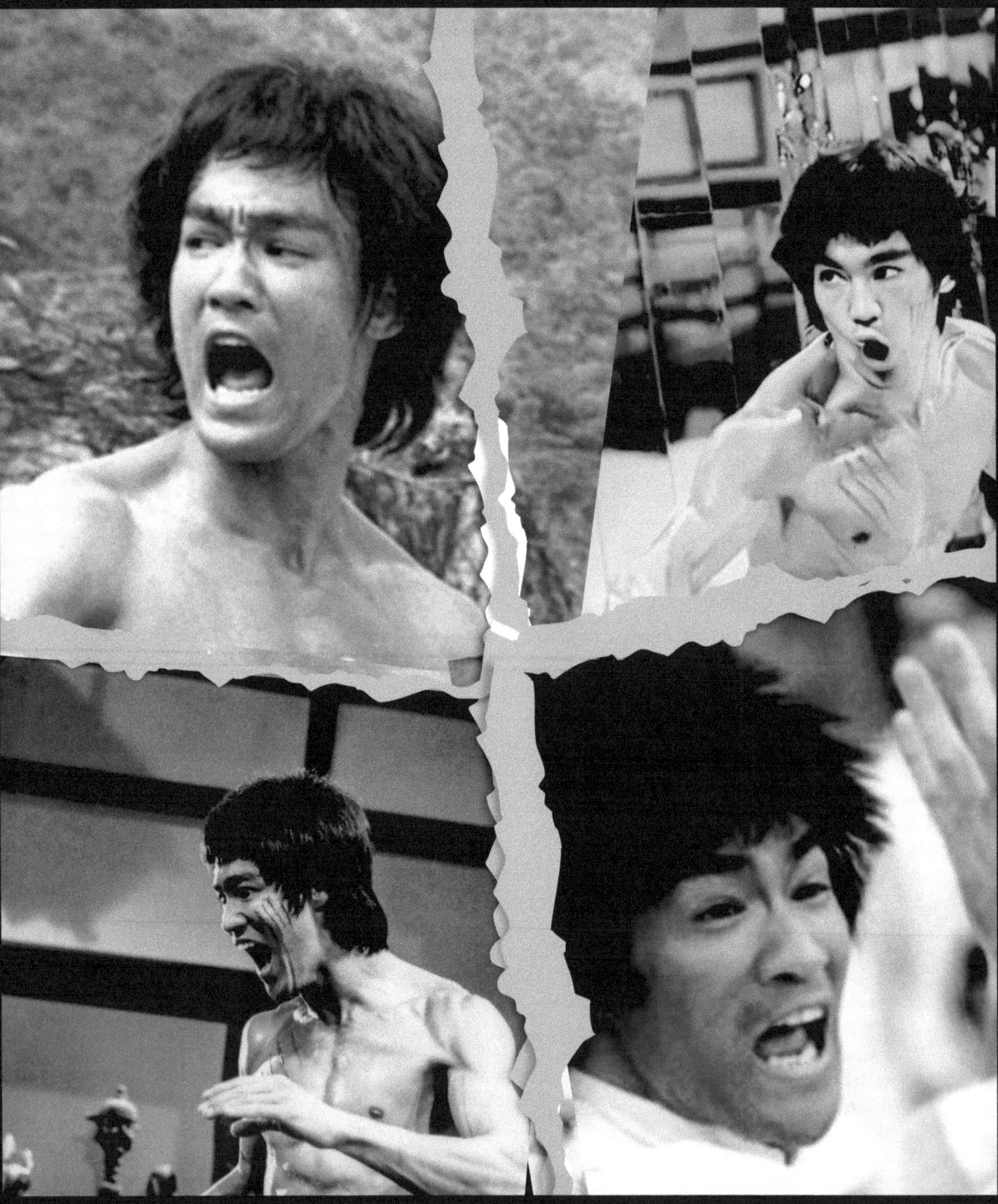

Lee's ability to express such a wide range of emotions with his face set him apart from many of his contemporaries and continues to be a benchmark for actors today. His expressive range has inspired countless performers who seek to emulate his ability to convey complex emotions without relying solely on dialogue. In today's cinema, where the subtleties of facial expression are crucial for storytelling, the influence of Bruce Lee's mastery is evident.

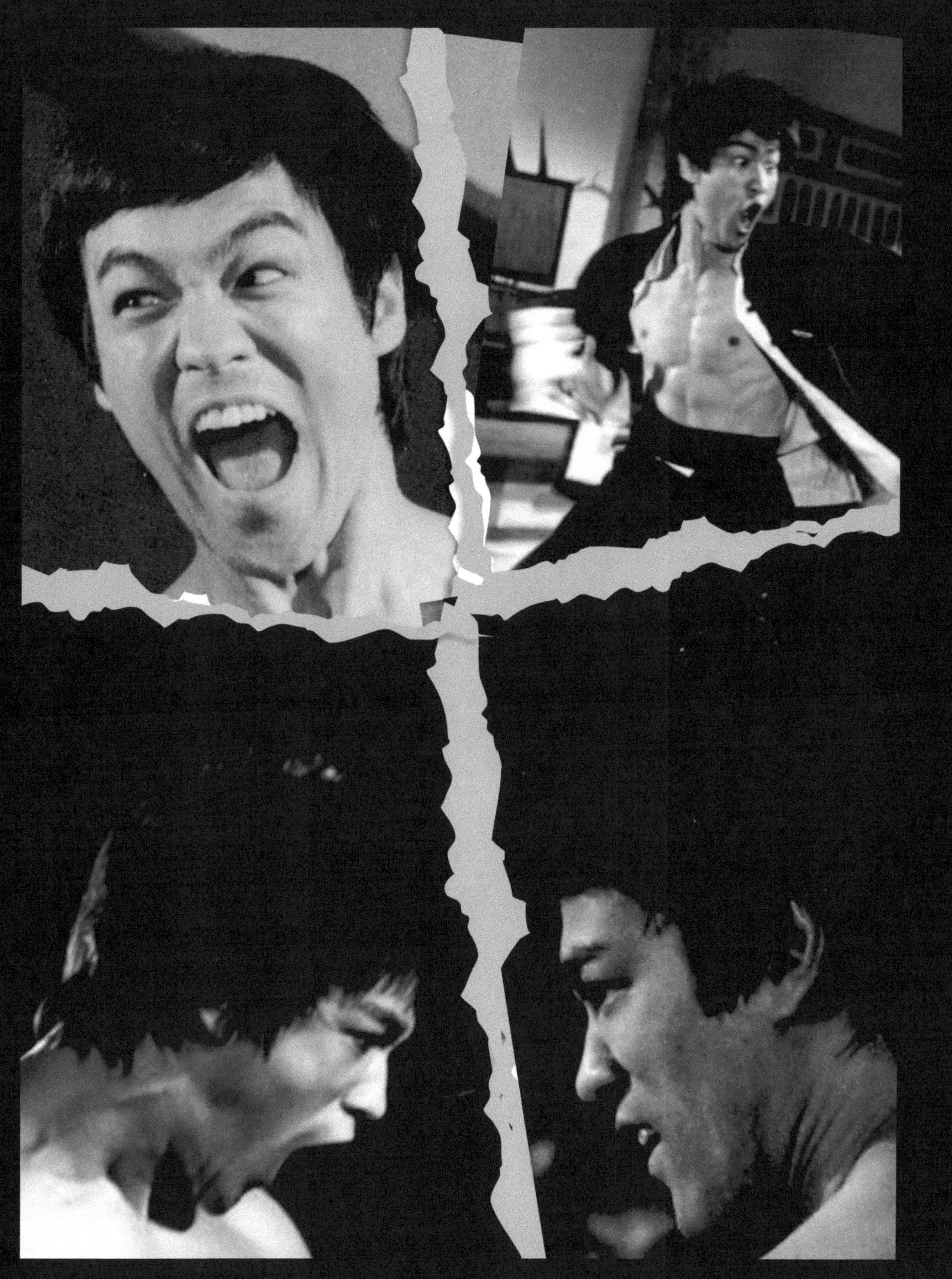

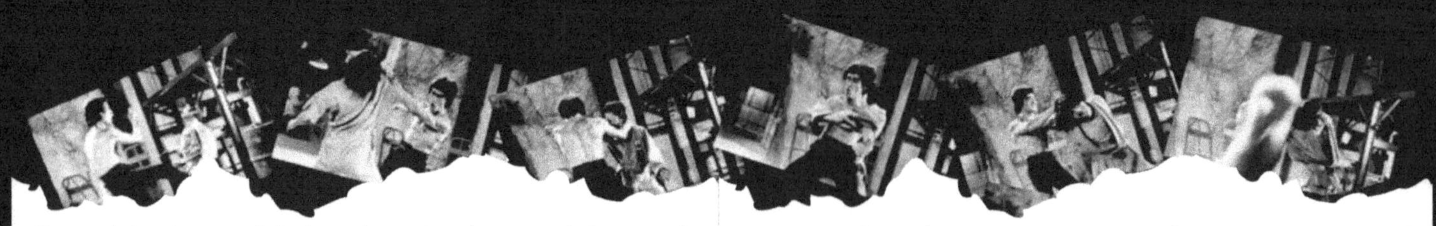

Transitioning to his iconic roles in martial arts cinema, Lee's face became a canvas for a vast array of emotions, each one as impactful as his lightning-fast kicks and punches. His pleasant smile, often seen in moments of camaraderie or triumph, was warm and infectious, revealing a side of Lee that was both relatable and endearing. This smile, disarming and genuine, contrasted sharply with the intensity he displayed during combat scenes, showcasing his versatility as an actor.

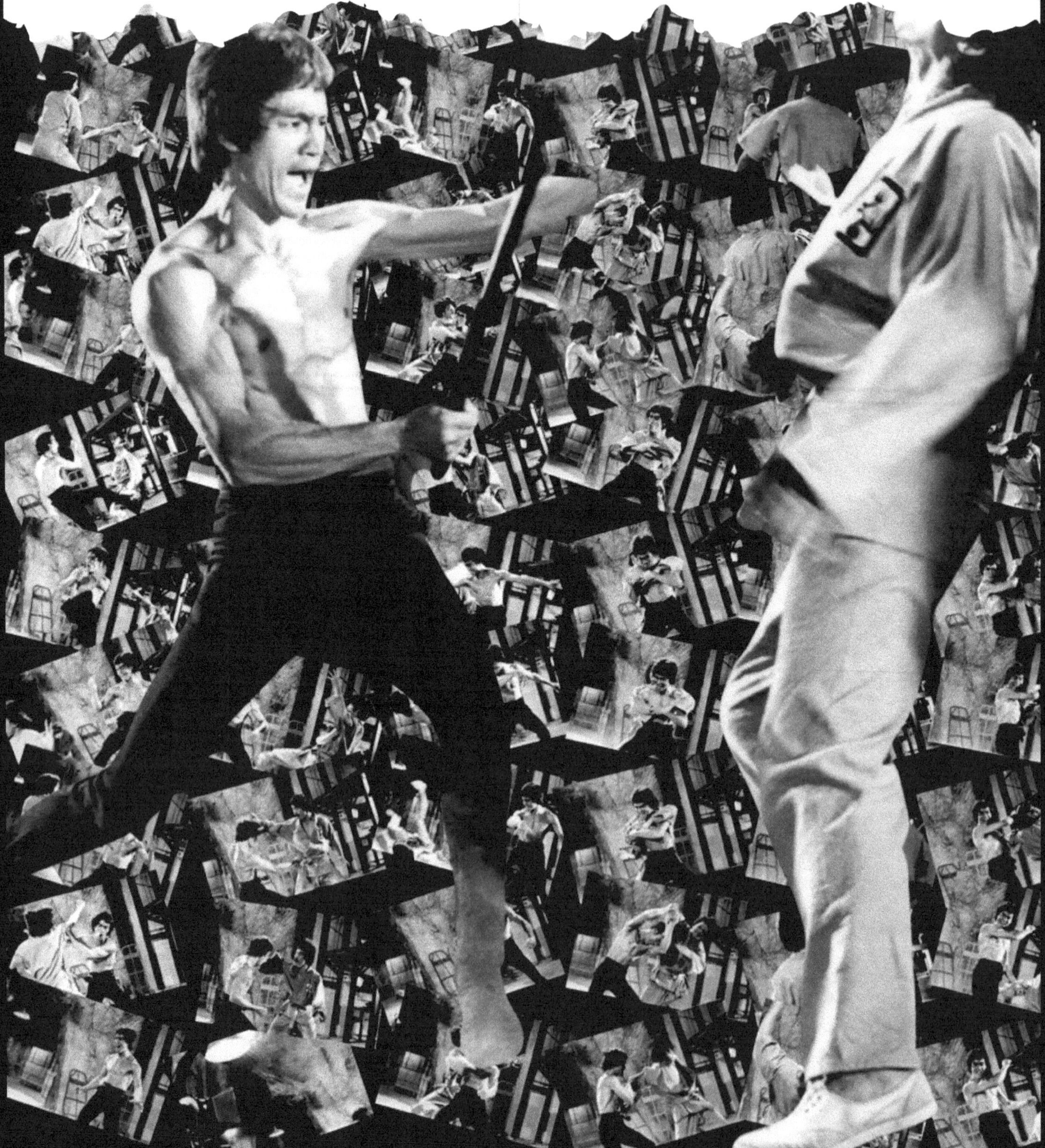

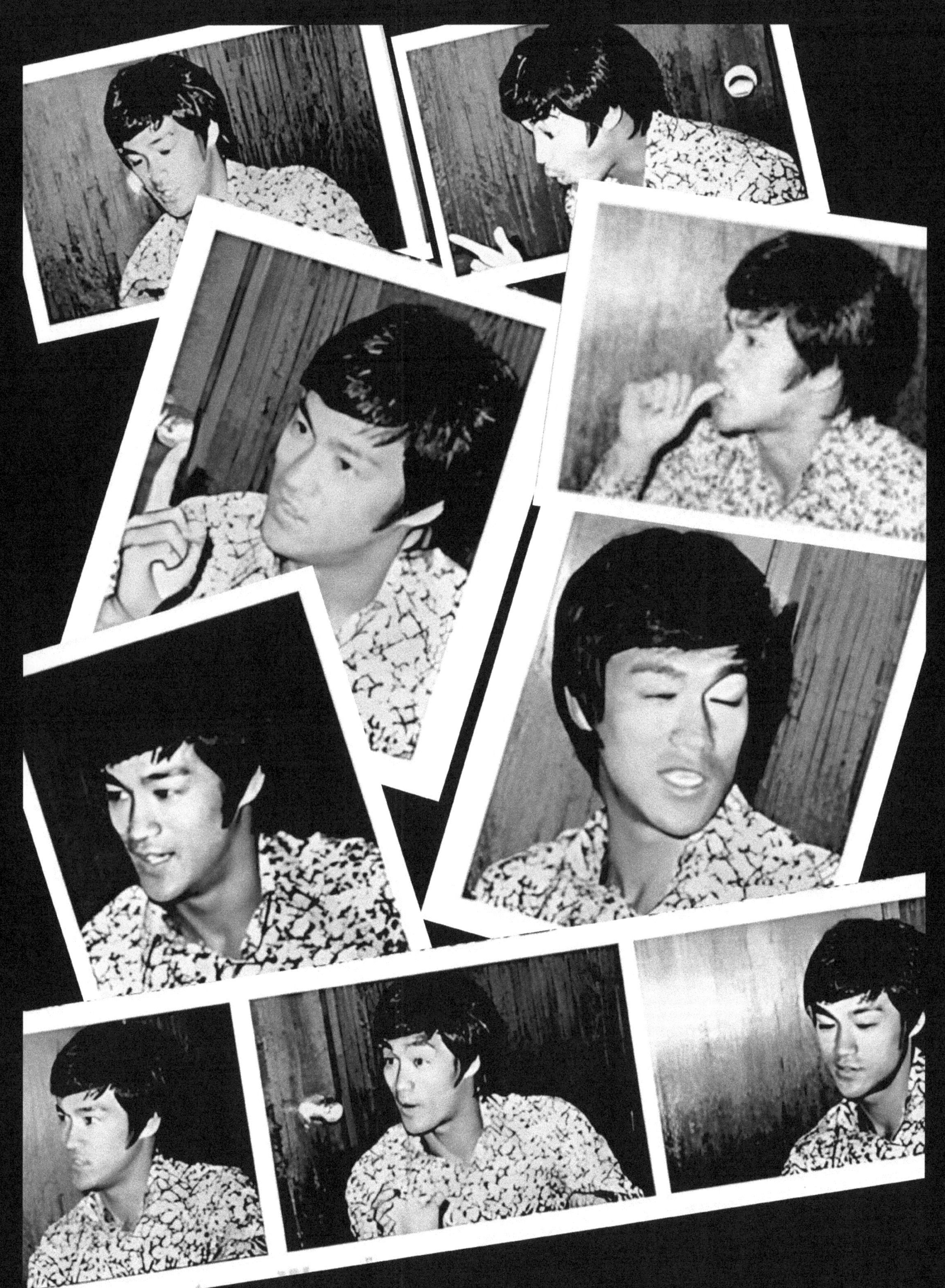

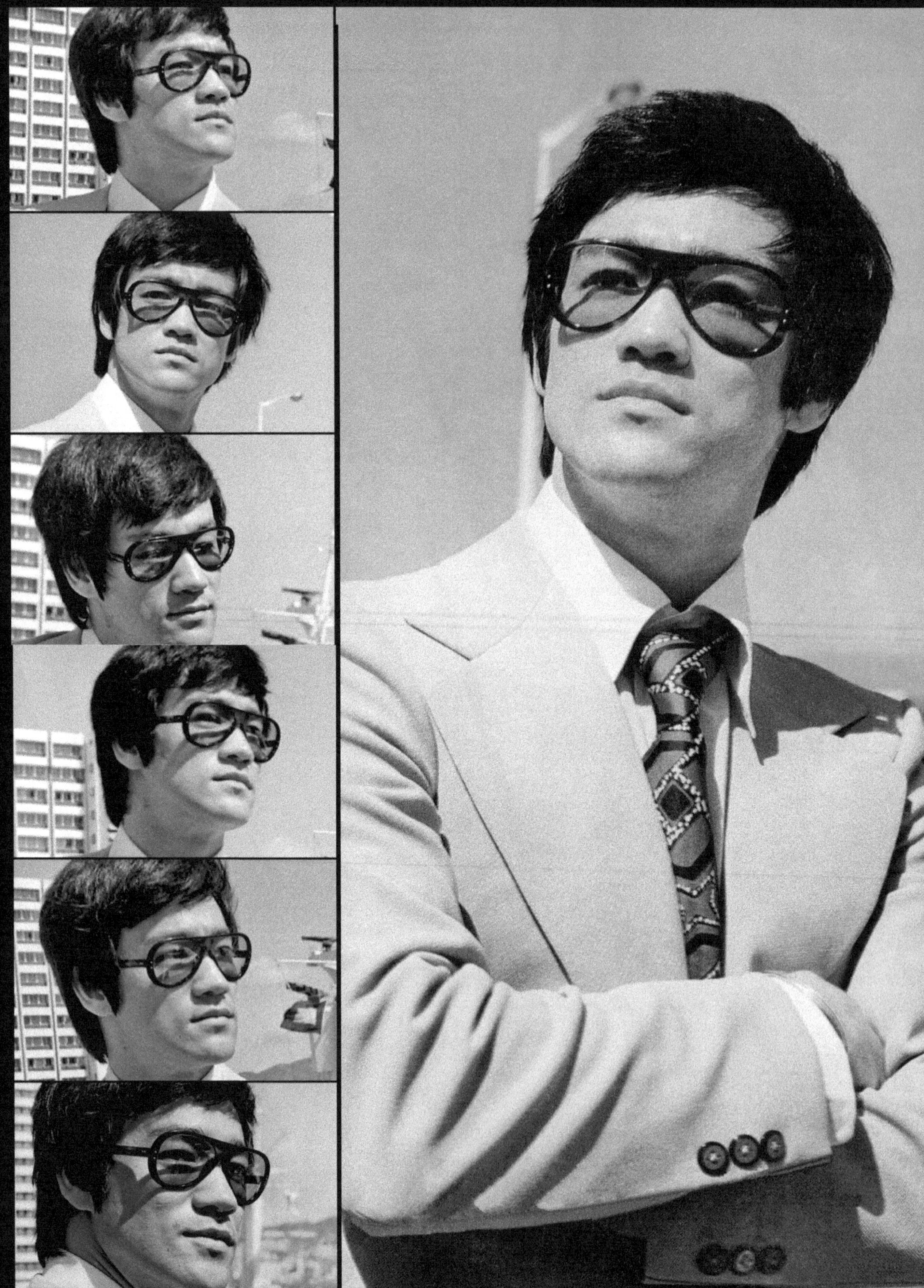

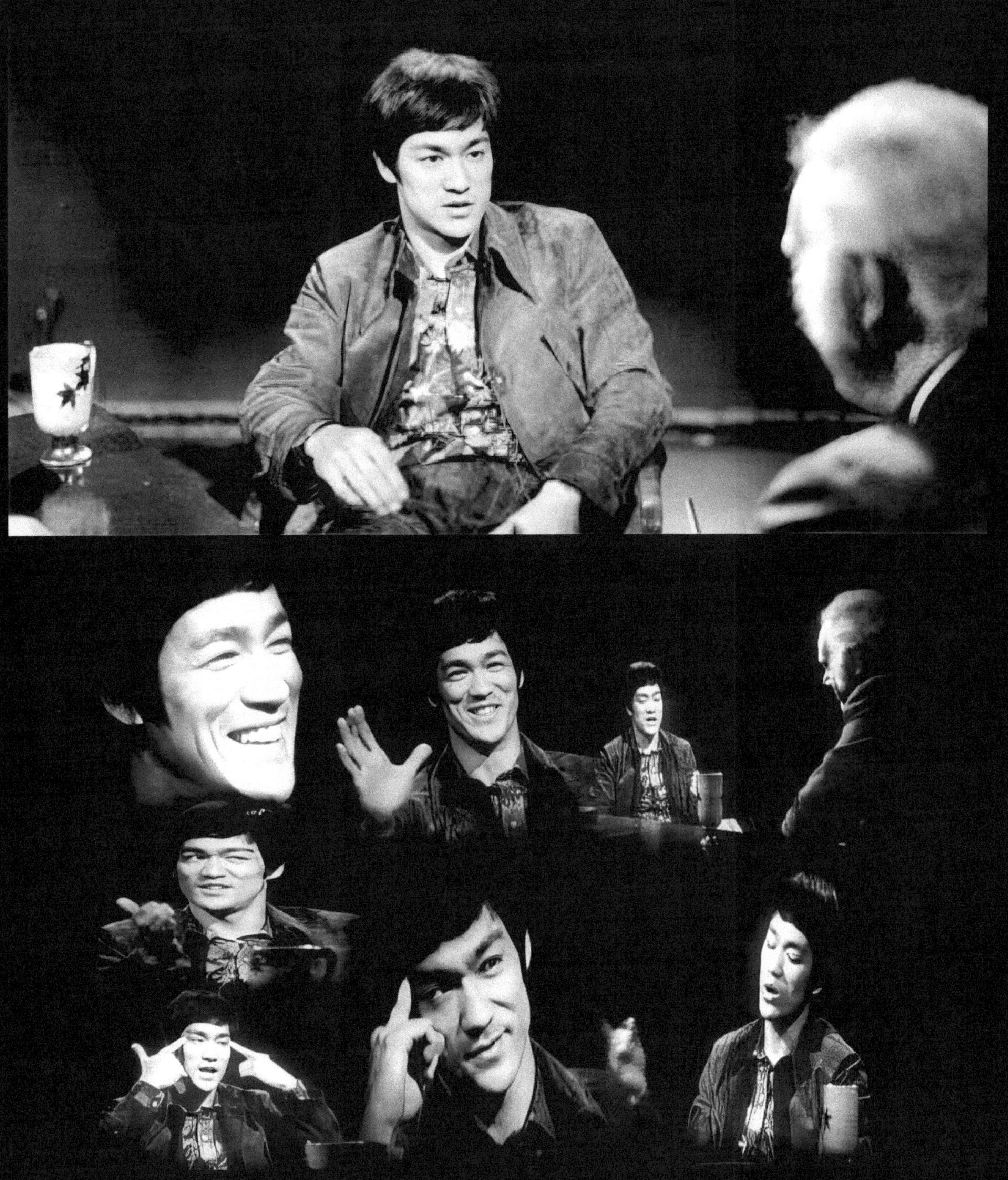

Bruce Lee: The Lost Interview refers to the 9 December 1971 edition of The Pierre Berton Show, featuring Bruce Lee's only English-language TV interview. Originally thought lost, it was rediscovered and aired on 2 November 1994. Filmed in Hong Kong, Lee discusses his career, martial arts philosophy, and the challenges of being an Asian actor in Hollywood. A review by Bill Stockey noted that the interview reveals Lee's more personal, approachable side.

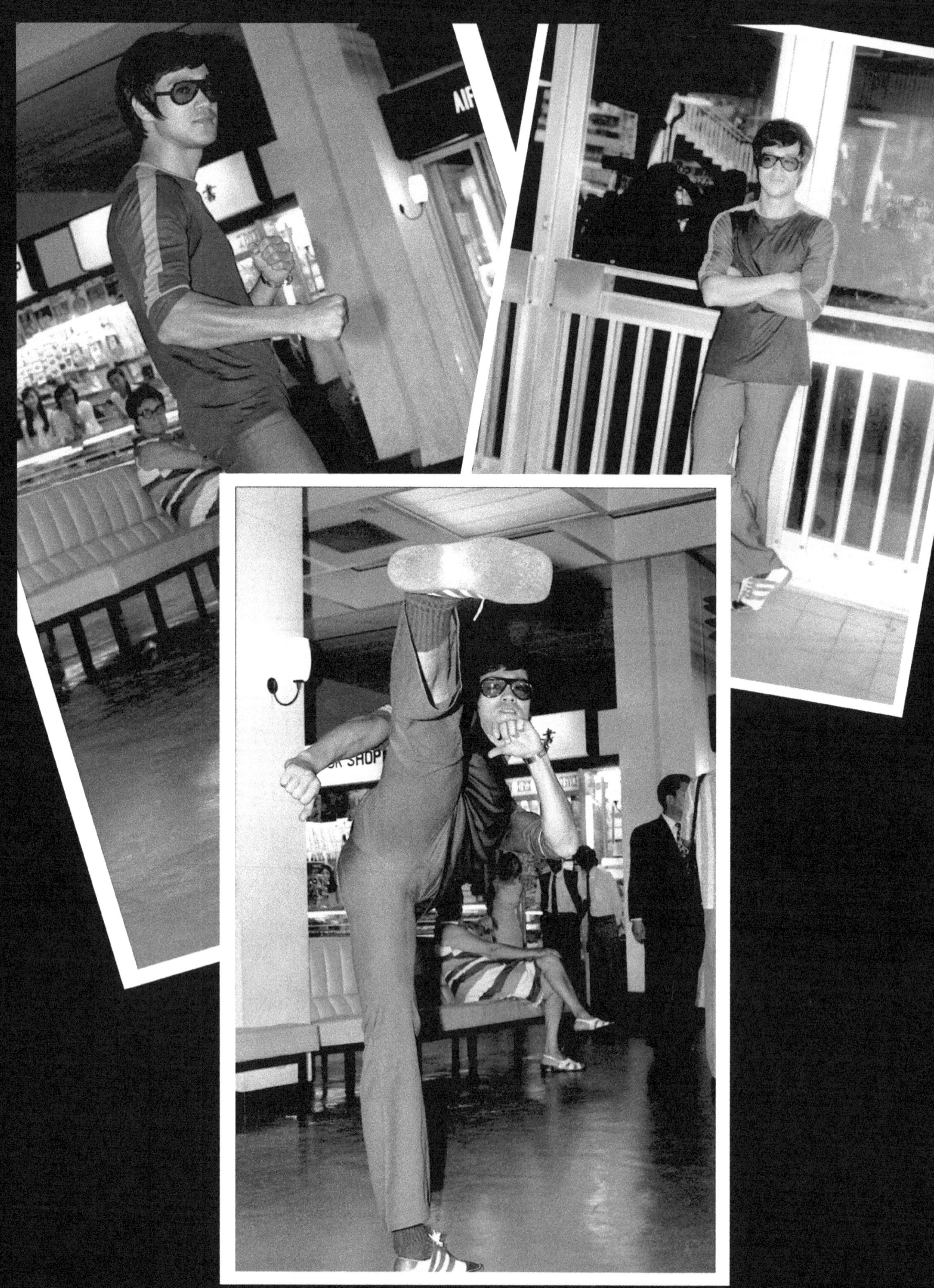

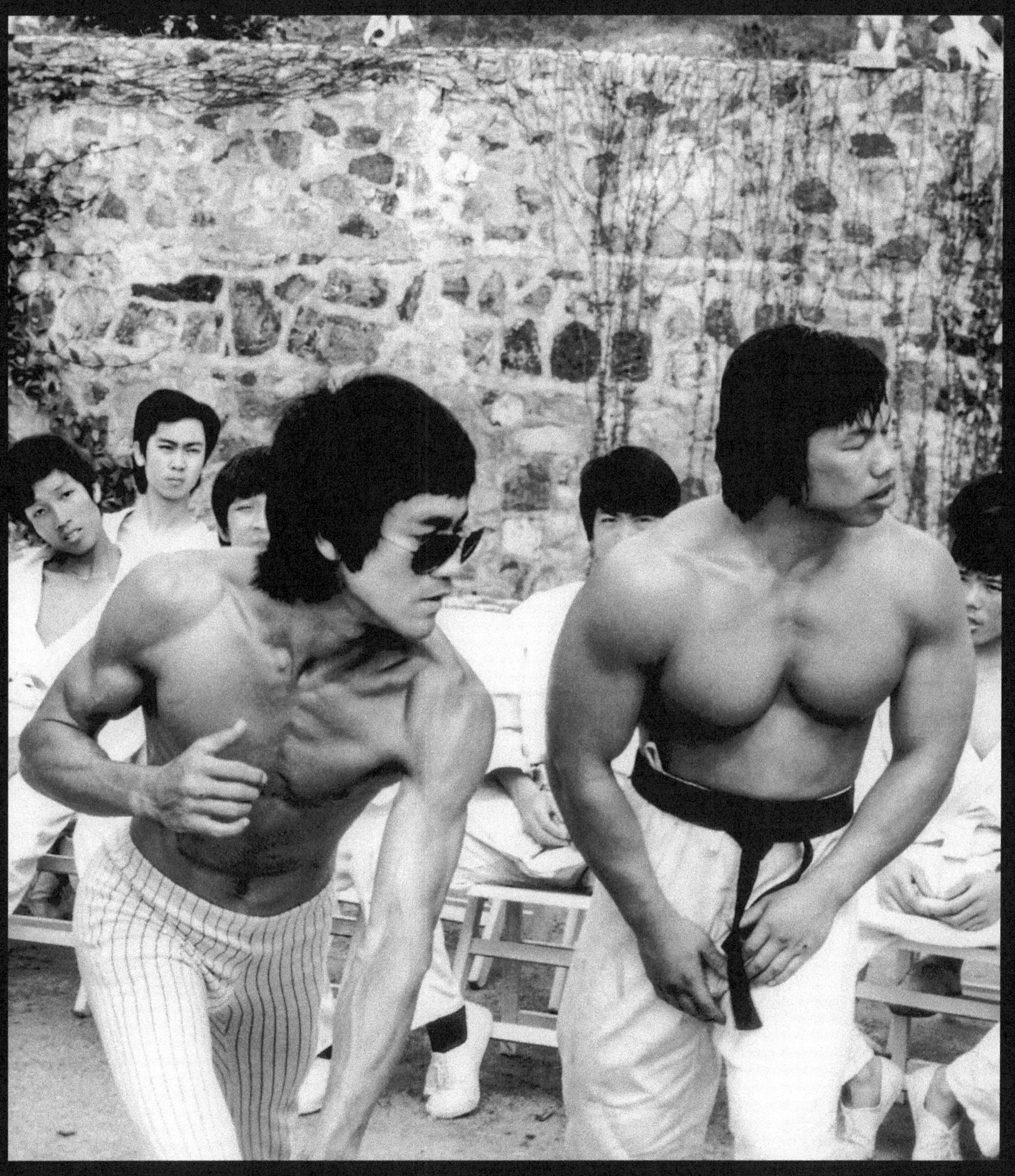

I HIT WITH SPEED, I HIT WITH POWER.
BUT ABOVE ALL, I HIT WITH EXPRESSION &
EMOTIONAL CONTENT

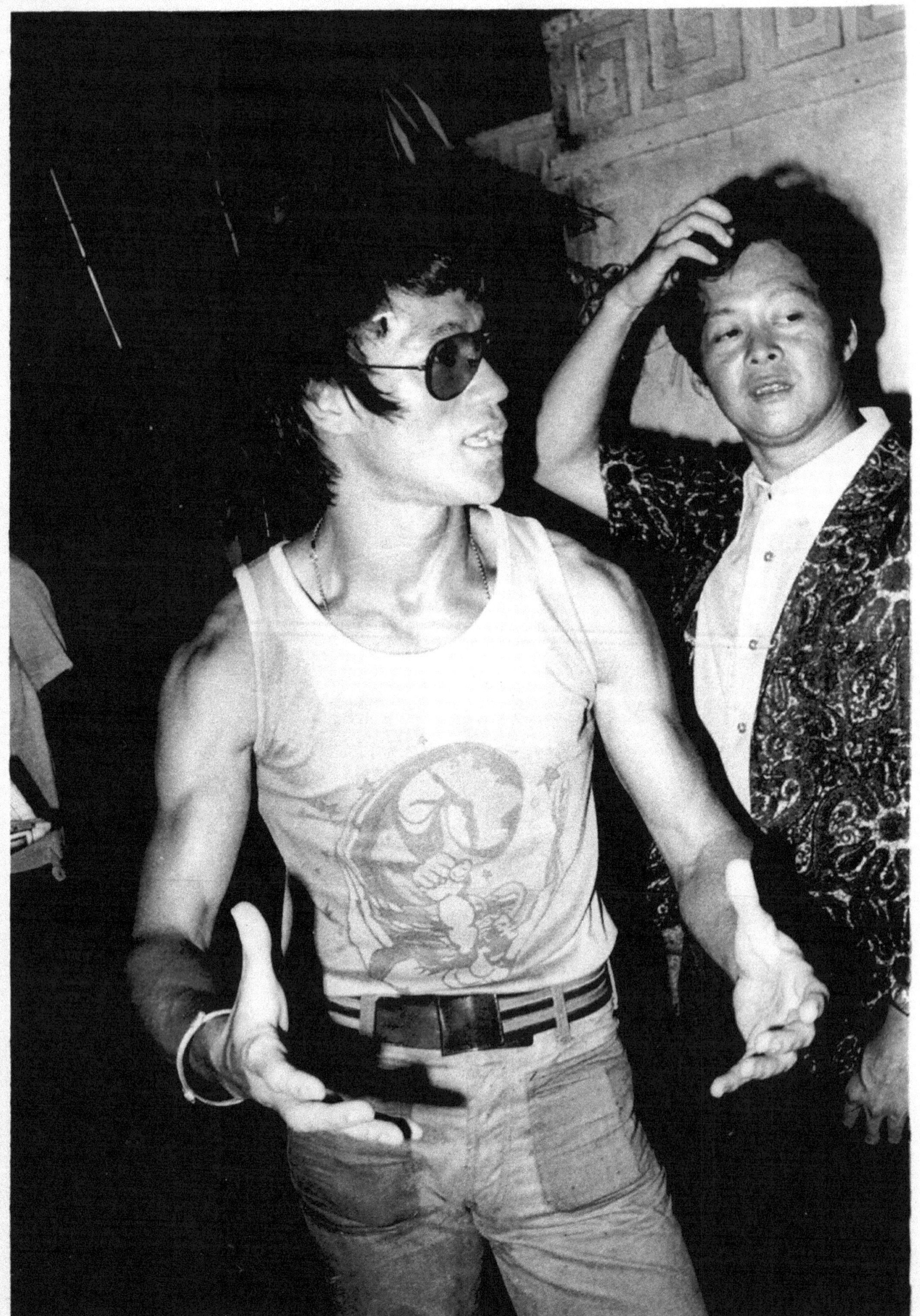

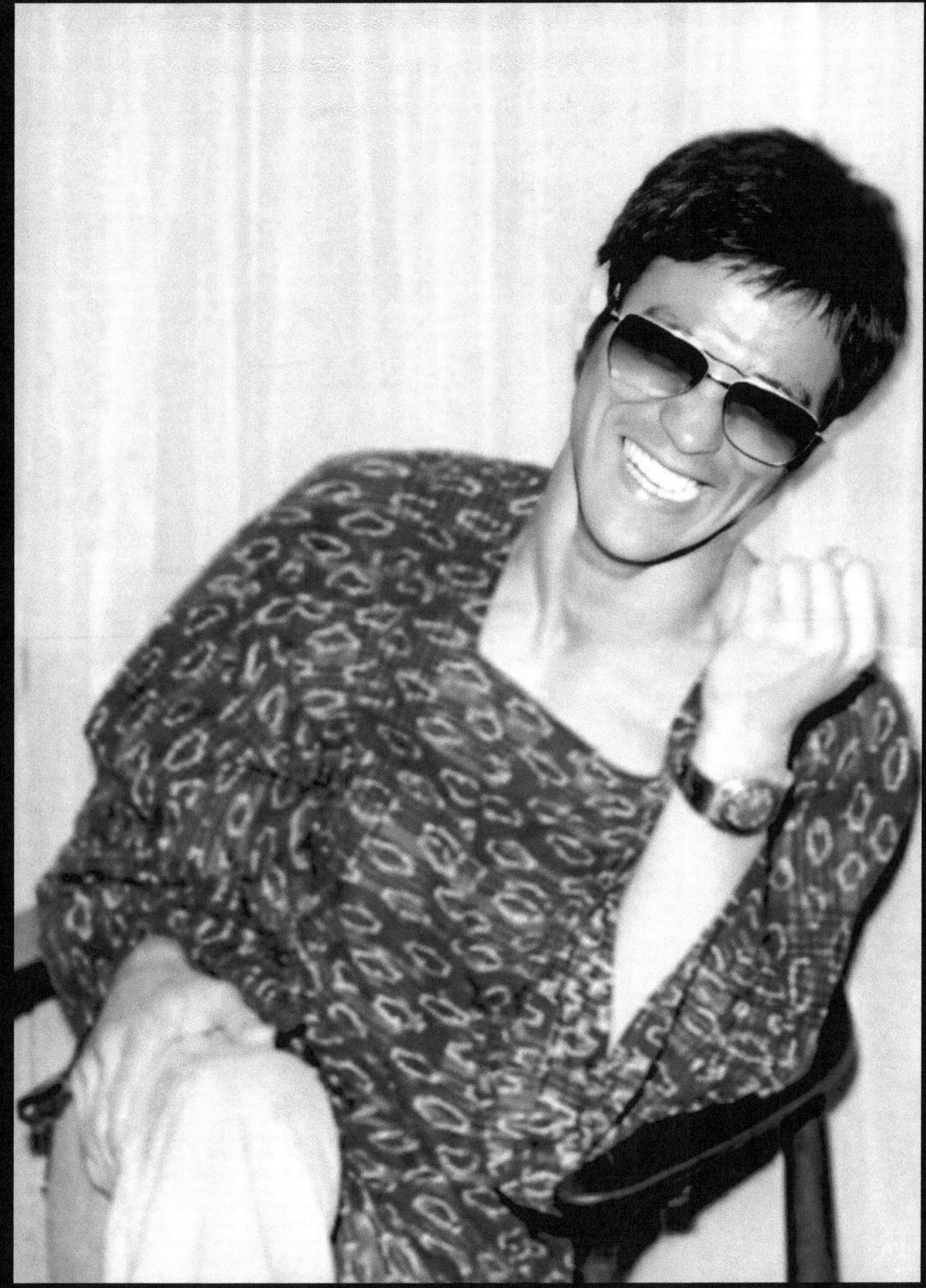

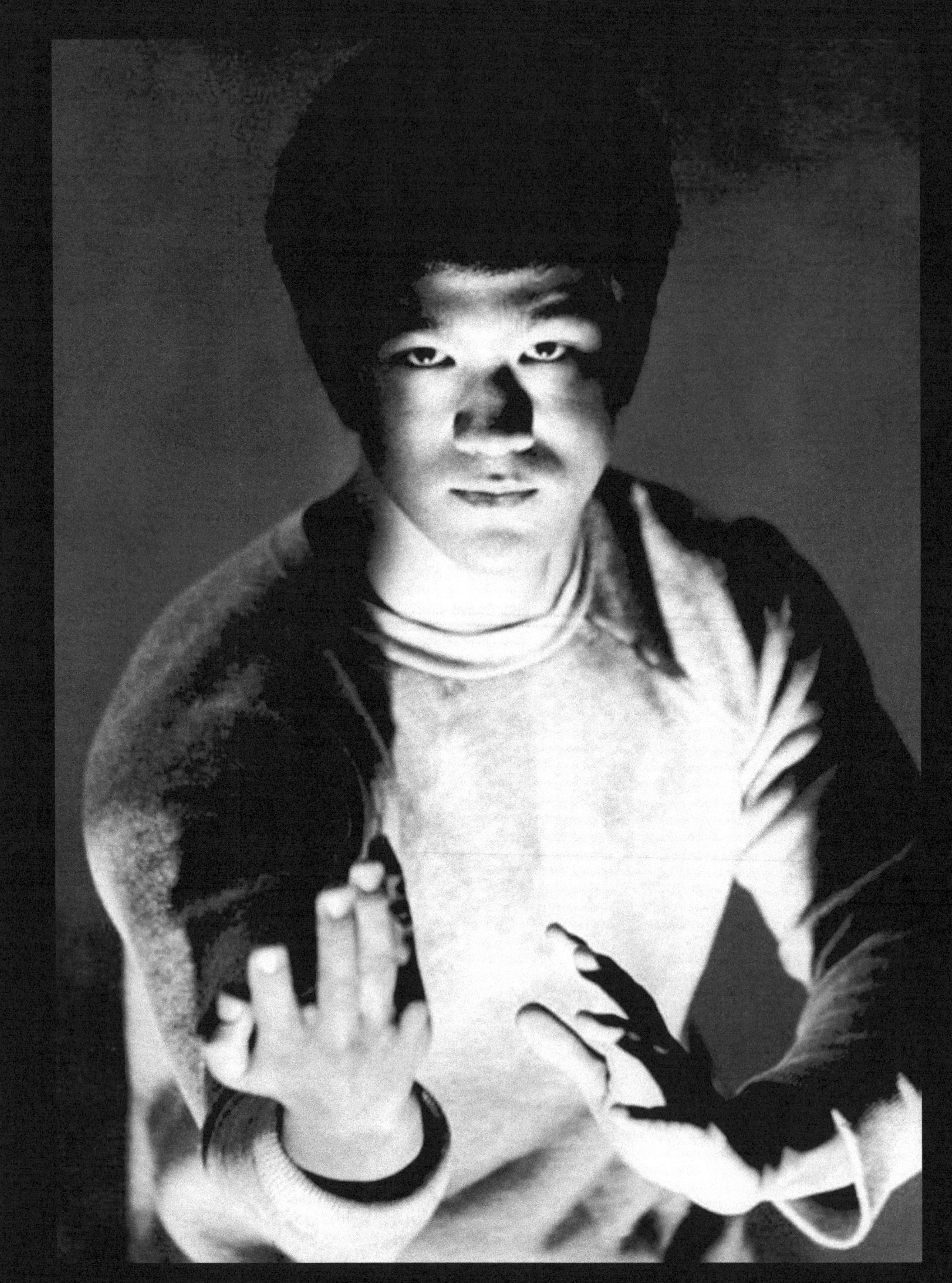

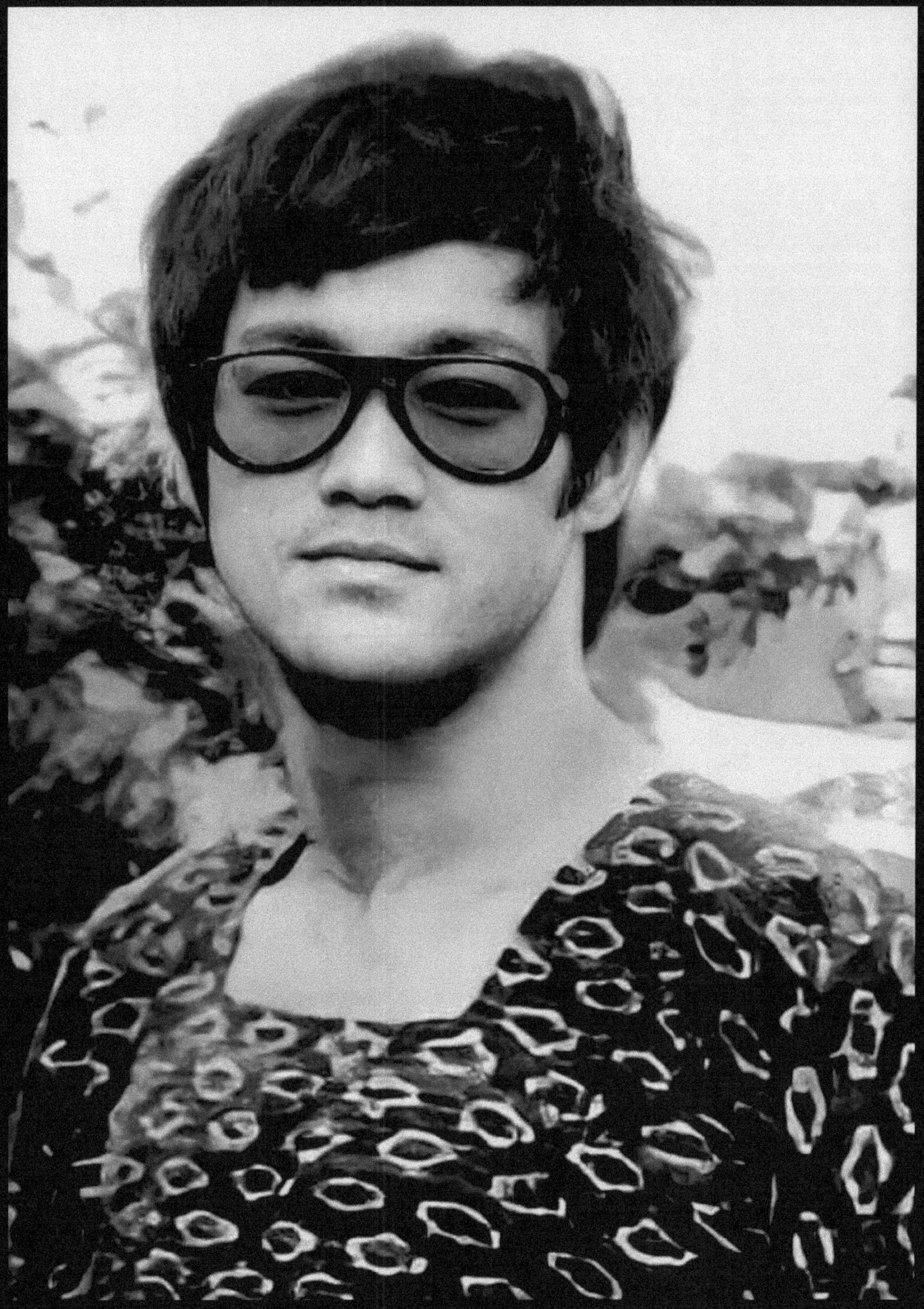

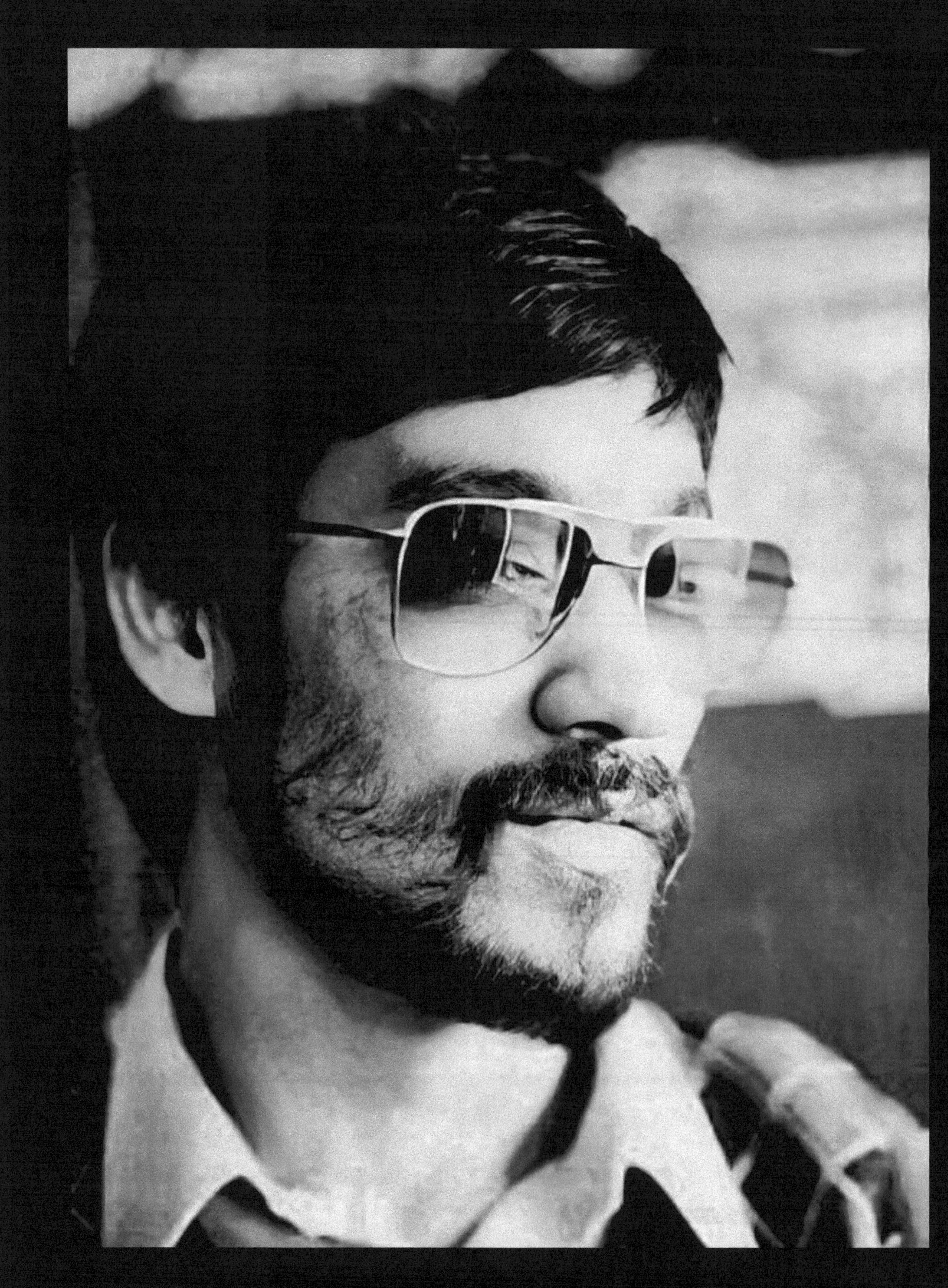

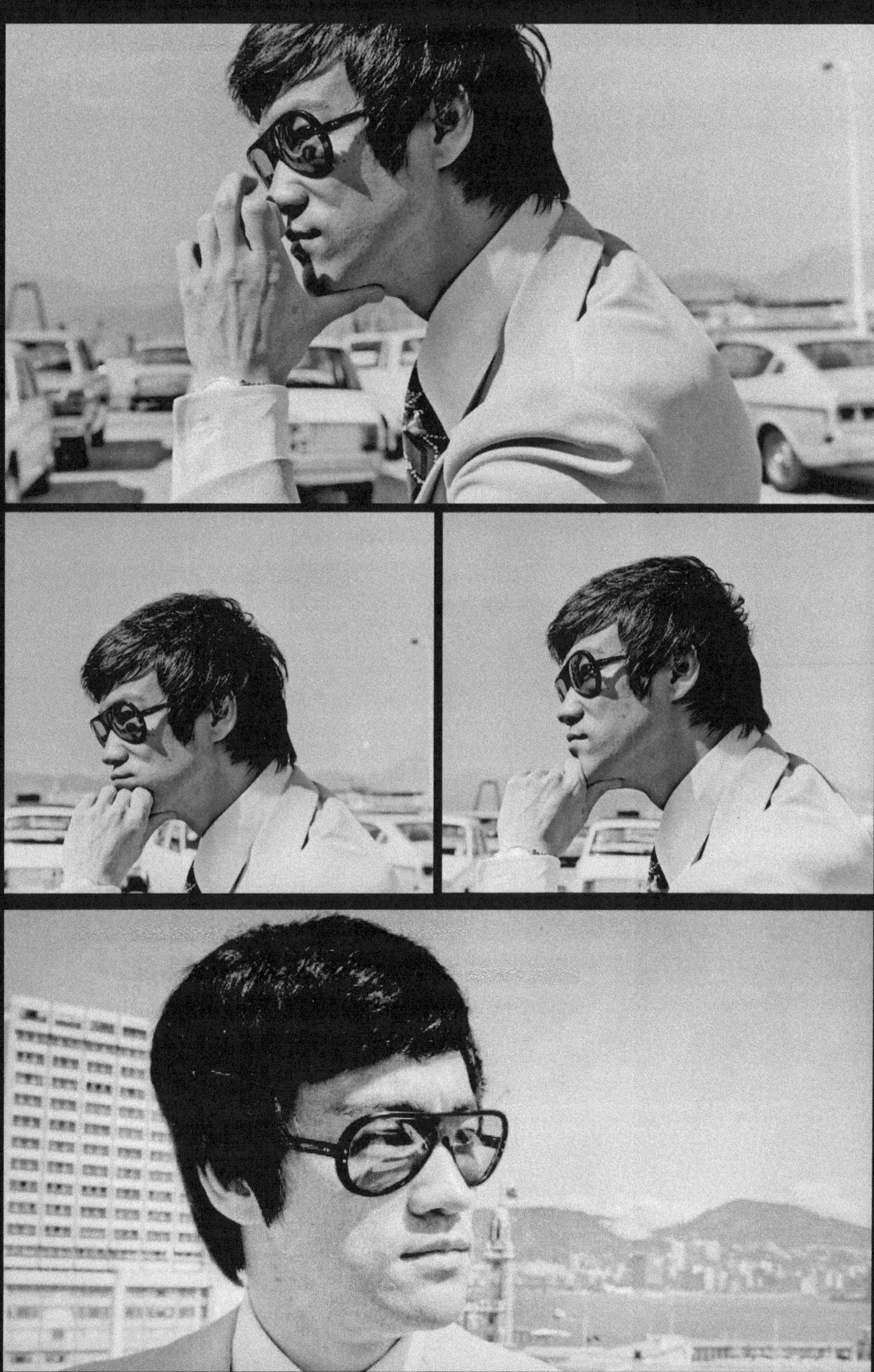

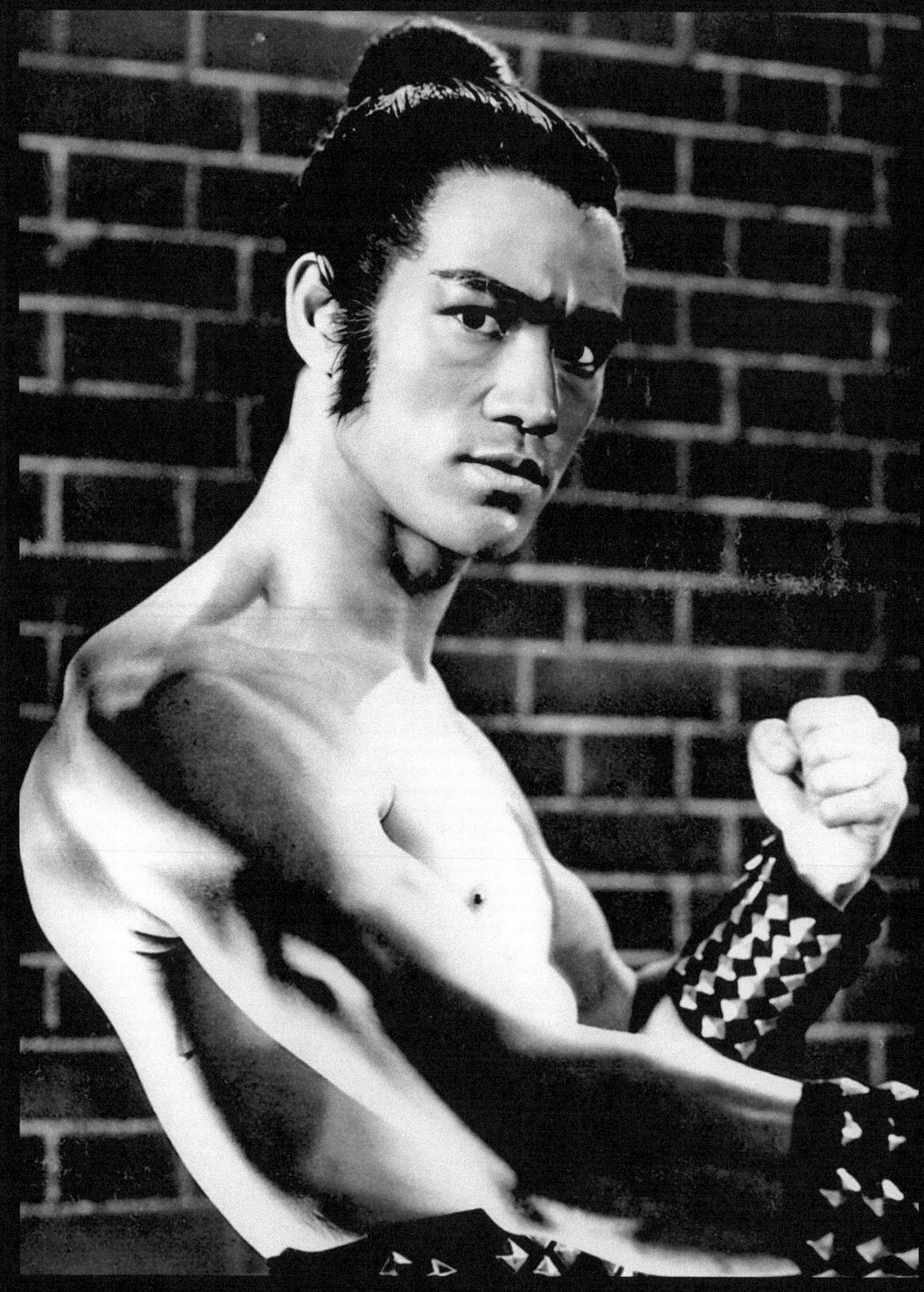

www.ingramcontent.com/pod-product-compliance
Lightning Source LLC
Chambersburg PA
CBHW040904070726
47599CB00038B/2298